GUIDELINES

FOR THE ECONOMIC ANALYSIS OF PROJECTS

YEARS

ADB

ASIAN DEVELOPMENT BANK

© 2017 Asian Development Bank
6 ADB Avenue, Mandaluyong City, 1550 Metro Manila, Philippines
Tel +63 2 632 4444; Fax +63 2 636 2444
www.adb.org; openaccess.adb.org

Some rights reserved. Published in 2017.
Printed in the Philippines.

ISBN 978-92-9257-763-6 (Print), 978-92-9257-764-3 (e-ISBN)
Publication Stock No. TIM178607-2
http://dx.doi.org/10.22617/TIM178607-2

Cataloging-In-Publication Data

Asian Development Bank.
          Guidelines for the economic analysis of projects.
Mandaluyong City, Philippines: Asian Development Bank, 2017.

1. Economic analysis of projects.   2. Cost-benefit analysis.
I. Asian Development Bank.

Notes:
In this publication, "$" refers to US dollars.
Corrigenda to ADB publications may be found at http://www.adb.org/publications/corrigenda

CONTENTS

APPENDIXES

TABLES AND FIGURES

FOREWORD

The Agreement Establishing the Asian Development Bank (ADB), also known as ADB Charter, requires that investment decisions on all loans made, guaranteed, or participated in by ADB are based on economic and efficiency considerations. Project economic analysis plays an important role in ensuring that the mandate of the Charter is met.

To ensure consistency in the approach to project economic analysis and to assist ADB staff and consultants with methodology, ADB issues guidelines for the conduct of project economic analysis. Such guidelines were last issued in 1997.

This publication presents revised guidelines. The revision responds to the changing development context and ADB operational priorities, as well as the recommendation for more methodological work in project economic analysis to support operational departments by ADB's Quality-at-Entry Assessments in recent years.

The revised guidelines incorporate a number of changes from the 1997 edition. First, the minimum required economic internal rate of return for investment decisions has been revised. Second, several issues that have emerged or become more important since the adoption of the 1997 edition are introduced, including economic analysis under various financing modalities, the treatment of the social cost of carbon, and economic analysis of regional economic cooperation projects. Third, a new chapter on benefit valuation by sector has been added, which details the method for valuing project benefits in major sectors of ADB operations. Fourth, appendixes have been updated. And fifth, the presentation of the guidelines has been made less technical and more user-friendly.

The guidelines provide general principles for the conduct of project economic analysis. The appendixes provide illustrations of their application. From time to time, ADB has published handbooks, technical reports, and other reference materials on project economic analysis which discuss sector-specific economic analysis in detail. The guidelines should be read together with those reference materials.

It is hoped that the revised guidelines will assist ADB staff and consultants to assess economic viability of bank operations for better quality-at-entry and greater development effectiveness.

Juzhong Zhuang
Deputy Chief Economist and Deputy Director General
Economic Research and Regional Cooperation Department
Asian Development Bank

ACKNOWLEDGMENTS

The revision of the guidelines was carried out by a team of staff of Economic Research and Regional Cooperation Department (ERCD). Juzhong Zhuang, ERCD's Deputy Chief Economist and Deputy Director General, led the team and took the overall responsibility in redrafting the main text and appendices, supported by Kee-Yung Nam, Utsav Kumar, and Maria Rowena M. Cham as core team members. Edimon Ginting, Director of Economic Analysis and Operational Support Division (EREA), and Cyn-Young Park, former EREA Director, provided coordination and support. Shang-Jin Wei, former Chief Economist and Director General of ERCD, provided guidance and inputs at various stages. Other EREA staff, including David Anthony Raitzer, Sakiko Tanaka, Valerie A. Mercer-Blackman, and Kaukab H. Naqvi, provided inputs to various chapters and appendices. Jindra Nuella Samson and Lilibeth Poot provided technical support. Aleli A. Rosario assisted in organizing the workshop for the finalization of the revised guidelines held in June 2016. Maria Melissa Gregorio-Dela Paz, Roslyn Perez and Gee Ann Carol D. Burac provided administrative and secretarial support.

The revision was supported by a number of ADB consultants. John Weiss, Emeritus Professor of Development Economics of University of Bradford, served as the lead consultant. Benoit Laplante provided inputs to economic valuation of nonmarket impacts. Damaris Yarcia supported the review of the social discount rate. Copy-editing was done by Tuesday Soriano, proofreading by Roslyn Perez and Ma. Regina Sibal; layout, cover design, and typesetting by Joe Mark Ganaban.

The revision of the guidelines benefited from valuable comments received from peer reviewers. Internal peer reviewers were David Dole and Muhammad Ehsan Khan. External peer reviewers included Glenn Jenkins, Queen's University and Eastern Mediterranean University; James Laird, Institute for Transport Studies, University of Leeds; and Ginés De Rus Mendoza, University of Las Palmas de Gran Canaria.

Detailed comments received during various rounds of interdepartmental reviews and ADB-wide consultations, in particular from departments of Central and West Asia, East Asia, Southeast Asia, South Asia, Pacific, Private Sector Operations,

Sustainable Development and Climate Change, Strategy and Policy, Operations Services and Financial Management, and Independent Evaluation; Office of General Counsel; and various sector and thematic groups, are gratefully acknowledged.

The team highly appreciates valuable feedback from participants at the finalization workshop, including ADB staff, external peer reviewers, and development partners from African Development Bank, European Investment Bank, Inter-American Development Bank, and World Bank, in particular, in the areas of social discount rate and social cost of carbon.

ABBREVIATIONS

ADB	–	Asian Development Bank
BCR	–	benefit–cost ratio
BPP	–	border parity price
CER	–	cost effectiveness ratio
CF	–	conversion factor
CIF	–	cost, insurance, and freight
CO_2	–	carbon dioxide
CPS	–	country partnership strategy
DALY	–	disability adjusted life years
DMC	–	developing member country
DMF	–	design and monitoring framework
EAL	–	emergency assistance loan
EIRR	–	economic internal rate of return
ENPV	–	economic net present value
FIL	–	financial intermediation loan
FIRR	–	financial internal rate of return
FOB	–	free on board
GHG	–	greenhouse gas
IRR	–	internal rate of return
NPV	–	net present value
QAE	–	quality-at-entry
SERF	–	shadow exchange rate factor
SWR	–	shadow wage rate
SWRF	–	shadow wage rate factor
TDH	–	transport, distribution, and handling
TVET	–	technical and vocational education and training
VOC	–	vehicle operating cost
WACC	–	weighted average cost of capital

I. INTRODUCTION

1.   The Agreement Establishing the Asian Development Bank (ADB Charter) requires staff to "take the necessary measures to ensure that the proceeds of any loan made, guaranteed or participated in by the Bank are used only for the purposes for which the loan was granted and with due attention to considerations of economy and efficiency" (Article 14.11). It also states that "only economic considerations shall be relevant to their decisions" (Article 36.2).[1] Project economic analysis is a key tool to ensure that ADB operations comply with the mandate of the ADB Charter and contribute to the broad objectives of poverty reduction, inclusive economic growth, environmental sustainability, and regional integration.

2.   Project economic analysis aims to ensure that scarce resources are allocated efficiently, and investment brings benefits to a country and raises the welfare of its citizens. All resource inputs used by a project have an opportunity cost because, without the project, they could create value elsewhere in the economy. An economically viable project requires that, first, it represents the least-cost or most efficient option to achieve the intended project outcomes; second, it generates an economic surplus above its opportunity cost; and third, it will have sufficient funds and the necessary institutional structure for successful operation and maintenance. ADB's development mandate also requires that an ADB-financed project distribute benefits and costs in a way consistent with its intended development objectives and that it can internalize the environmental effects.

3.   The guidelines outlined in this publication set a general approach to the economic analysis of projects for application by ADB. They are a revised version of the edition published in 1997. The revisions respond to the findings of ADB's economic analysis retrospectives and quality-at-entry (QAE) assessments in recent years, which highlight the weaknesses in project economic analysis as applied in ADB operations. One of the recommendations was that more methodological work be carried out to guide ADB staff and consultants for better QAE. The revisions also consider the changing development context and ADB operational priorities, as well as methodological developments in project economic analysis.

4.   The revised guidelines incorporate a number of changes from the 1997 edition. First, the minimum required economic internal rate of return (EIRR) for investment decisions has been revised. Second, several issues that have emerged or become more important since the adoption of the 1997 edition are introduced, including economic analysis under various financing modalities, the treatment of the social cost of carbon, and economic analysis of regional economic cooperation

---

[1]   ADB. 1965. *Agreement Establishing the Asian Development Bank*. Manila.

projects. Third, a new chapter on benefit valuation by sector has been added, which details the method for valuing project benefits in major sectors of ADB operations. Fourth, appendixes have been updated. And fifth, the presentation of the guidelines has been made less technical and more user-friendly.

5.   ADB's project portfolio now covers a wide range of sectors, encompassing physical infrastructure and social sectors and both public and private sector operations. The purpose of the guidelines is to provide general principles of project economic analysis, which should be read in conjunction with various handbooks, technical reports, and other reference materials on project economic analysis that have been produced by ADB and which give more detailed guidance relating to appraisal in individual sectors. A list of these is provided in Appendix 1.

II. SCOPE OF PROJECT ECONOMIC ANALYSIS

6.   A well-conducted economic analysis should show that (i) a project is in line with the development context of a borrowing country and ADB's country partnership strategy (CPS); (ii) there is strong rationale for the public sector and ADB to finance the project; and (iii) the selected project represents the most efficient or least-cost option among all the feasible alternatives for achieving the intended project benefits and, when benefit can be valued, it will generate a positive economic net present value (ENPV) using the minimum required economic internal rate of return (EIRR) as the discount rate, i.e., the project has an EIRR higher than the discount rate.

A.   Key Areas of Economic Analysis

7.   Economic analysis involves analyzing a number of issues related to the economic viability of a project. In ADB, these analyses are carried out at different stages of a project operational cycle (Figure 1).

Country context analysis

8.   A project cannot be isolated from the wider development context of a borrowing country. Country context analysis looks at the development constraints of a developing member country (DMC) and how the proposed project can contribute to a DMC's development objectives. It explains where the project fits in the DMC's development plan and ADB's CPS. It also examines how the economy of the borrowing country is likely to evolve over a project's life and how changes in

Figure 1: Project Economic Analysis at ADB—Key Areas and Operational Cycle

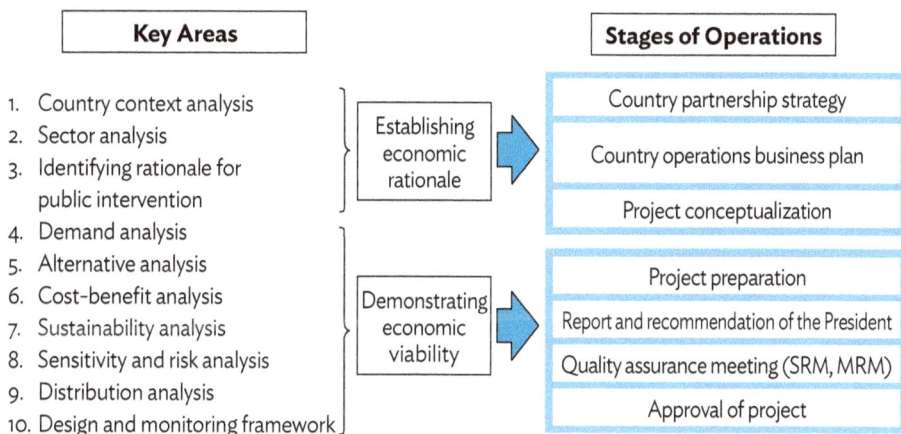

Key Areas		Stages of Operations
1. Country context analysis 2. Sector analysis 3. Identifying rationale for public intervention	Establishing economic rationale	Country partnership strategy Country operations business plan Project conceptualization
4. Demand analysis 5. Alternative analysis 6. Cost-benefit analysis 7. Sustainability analysis 8. Sensitivity and risk analysis 9. Distribution analysis 10. Design and monitoring framework	Demonstrating economic viability	Project preparation Report and recommendation of the President Quality assurance meeting (SRM, MRM) Approval of project

MRM = Management Review Meeting, SRM = Staff Review Meeting.
Source: ADB Economic Research and Regional Cooperation Department.

key macroeconomic indicators—such as the exchange rate, interest rates, and the government budget position—may impact on a project. Country context analysis should be carried out as part of CPS, country operations and business plan (COBP), or project conceptualization.

Sector analysis

9. Sector analysis is critical to understanding binding constraints to the effective functioning of a concerned sector, why a project is proposed, and how it will help address the sector constraints. Sector constraints can be related to policy and incentives, the relevant legal and regulatory framework, or physical infrastructure. In cases where public enterprises are the primary provider of goods and services, the performance, management, and financial sustainability of these enterprises; the adequacy of fiscal allocation to the sector; and the government's sector development plan should be assessed. Sector analysis should be carried out as part of CPS, COBP, or project conceptualization.

10. Sector analysis also involves the examination of (i) current and future demand; (ii) existing sources of supply, their costs, and any intended investment that may compete with the project; (iii) the contribution of the proposed project to sector demand, cost reduction, or technological innovation; (iv) the extent of direct government involvement in the sector either as a producer or financier and any

government subsidy to or taxation of the sector; and (v) whether additional physical investment embodied in the project under consideration is the best solution to the problem at hand.

Identifying the rationale for public involvement

11.   The case for public support in the form of ADB funding should be set out as part of the initial assessment of a project (in the CPS, the COBP, or the project concept). A clear economic rationale for public sector involvement helps to narrow the range of alternative ways of addressing a development problem. Public intervention is justified when a market fails to deliver goods and services efficiently. Market failures can arise from various factors such as increasing returns to scale, externalities, asymmetric information, unspecified property rights, coordination failures, and specific characteristics of certain public goods that make their use non-rival and non-excludable.

12.   When the private sector fails to produce a socially optimal level of output, public sector involvement is justified. The public sector may use public ownership as a means of providing goods and services. Alternatively, public sector involvement can take the form of providing financing or fiscal incentives, such as subsidies or tax credits, while leaving the private sector to produce the required output. Economic analysis should justify both the choice of public involvement and the form it takes. Where goods and services are produced in relatively monopolized markets, ADB funding of a new project should be combined with the development of a legal and regulatory framework. Where ADB finances private sector operations, the justification for this with regard to the additionality brought by ADB funding should be made clear.

Demand analysis

13.   As part of project preparation or feasibility study, demand analysis establishes the existing and future consumer demand for goods and services to be produced by a project and provides a basis for estimating the project's economic benefits. A project that fails to attract an adequate level of demand for its output, at an appropriate price, will not be operating efficiently and will create a misuse of scarce resources. Market research and user surveys can be used to estimate demand at different price levels. Project demand should also be assessed in the context of the likely total future demand for and supply of the product to establish how far the project will take market share from existing producers and whether its output will have an impact on the market price. Decisions on project scale should allow for the impact of proposed tariffs on the level and timing of project demand.

Alternative analysis

14. Economic efficiency requires that the proposed project represents the most efficient option among available feasible alternatives for addressing the identified problem. In many cases, this means that the selected project should have the lowest discounted cost per unit of output or outcome. However, when project alternatives have very different benefit flows, for example, because of quality differences, alternative analysis cannot be based on the cost comparison alone, and the most efficient project option is the one with the highest ENPV, provided that its investment is within budget. In some cases, alternative analysis may be supplemented by multi-criteria analysis,[2] depending on the data available. Alternative analysis should be carried out as part of project preparation.

Cost–benefit analysis

15. Estimating economic benefits and costs associated with the proposed project requires establishing the with project and without project scenarios and comparing the two. The without project scenario is not necessarily the business-as-usual case, as there may be instances where the current position is untenable and some steps toward mitigation are needed even without the proposed project. Monetary values of project benefits and costs, associated with outputs and inputs, must be identified in the years in which they arise. Any external effects affecting the rest of the economy but not reflected in market transactions by the project itself—such as adverse or beneficial environmental impacts—where they can be identified, must also be included.

16. The ENPV and the EIRR should be calculated for all projects in which benefits can be valued. The general criterion for accepting a project is achieving a positive ENPV discounted at the minimum required EIRR, or achieving the minimum required EIRR. ADB's newly adopted minimum required EIRR is 9%. However, for social sector projects, selected poverty-targeting projects (such as rural roads and rural electrification), and projects that primarily generate environmental benefits

---

[2] Multi-criteria analysis (MCA) is a tool used to assess the different investment alternatives available to achieve a given set of outcomes. Typically, the appraiser would have a predefined set of criteria that are aligned to the intended outcomes of the proposed investment, with weights assigned to each criterion. In cases where standard cost-benefit analysis or cost-effectiveness analysis is not possible or inadequate, MCA helps to decide the most preferred option among investment alternatives with clearly laid-out criteria and transparency. For more details on MCA in the context of project economic analysis, see European Investment Bank. 2013. *The Economic Appraisal of Investment Projects at the EIB.* http://www.eib.org/attachments/thematic/economic_appraisal_of_investment_projects_en.pdf; and European Commission. 2014. *Guide to Cost–Benefit Analysis of Investment Projects.* Brussels.

(such as pollution control, protection of the ecosystem, flood control, and control of deforestation), the minimum required EIRR can be lowered to 6%. Where a project's benefits cannot be adequately quantified in monetary terms, its cost-effectiveness must be demonstrated as part of alternative analysis.

Sustainability analysis

17.   Economic viability requires that a project is designed such that its net economic benefits are sustained during the project's economic life. This includes demonstration of the financial and institutional sustainability of a project. Assessing financial sustainability requires two types of analysis: financial evaluation of the project and financial analysis of the project-executing and/or implementing entity. The former focuses on the ability of the project to generate sufficient incremental cash flows to cover its financial costs (capital and recurrent costs). In this regard, analysis of the cost-recovery objectives and mechanisms of the project is important. Without full cost recovery, a financial evaluation will be meaningless. In the case of full cost recovery, the financial net present value discounted at the project's weighted average cost of capital (WACC) must be greater than zero, and the financial internal rate of return (FIRR) must be greater than WACC. Financial analysis of the project-executing and/or implementing entity aims to evaluate whether the concerned entity is financially robust enough to undertake the project and operate and maintain the project assets. This involves assessing the ability of the entity to operate as a going concern, to operate and maintain the entire network of assets including the project, and to fund recurrent costs.[3] The institutional capacity of the project-operating entity to implement the project should also be assessed.

18.   To address environmental concerns, a project should pay the full cost for its use of natural and environmental resources and, where this causes long-term environmental damage, be required to undertake appropriate expenditure for mitigation. Similarly, the environmental benefits created by a project need to be valued and included in the project economic analysis. A project can also be affected by the environment effects, and ADB policy now requires that climate-proofing issues be considered in project design to minimize the negative impact of long-term environmental effects, such as droughts, soil erosion, or floods, on projects. The economic benefits from ancillary investment designed to protect the project from potential climatic change must be assessed and compared with the cost of this protection.[4]

---

[3]   See ADB Operations Manual, Section G2. *Financial Management, Cost Estimates, Financial Analysis, and Financial Performance Indicators.*
[4]   See ADB. 2015. *Economic Analysis of Climate-Proofing Investment Projects.* Manila.

Risk and sensitivity analysis

19.   Project economic analysis should highlight the factors that are important to the success of the project but subject to risk, the sources of risk, and possible mitigating measures. Sensitivity analysis must assess the impact of changing values of the different parameters on project outcome. Switching values—showing the change in a parameter required for the project decision to shift from acceptance to rejection— should be presented for key parameters. Project economic analysis may draw on ex post evaluation results for similar projects to assess the likelihood of these switching values actually occurring. For projects that involve large investment, a quantitative risk analysis applying a probability distribution to key variables can be applied.

Distribution analysis

20.   Assessing how far different stakeholder groups gain or lose from a project should also be part of economic analysis. Where a project is targeted at a particular social group, it will be important to assess the proportion of project benefits that go to this group. It is also important to assess who bears the project cost and how far the incentives implied by the income changes identified in the distribution analysis are compatible with the assumptions in the project's design and monitoring framework (DMF).

B.   Difference between Economic Analysis and Financial Evaluation

21.   Project economic analysis and financial evaluation both involve the identification of project benefits and costs during the years in which they occur and converting all future cash flows to their present value using the technique of discounting. Both analyses generate net present value (NPV) and internal rate of return (IRR) indicators, termed economic NPV (ENPV) and economic IRR (EIRR) in the case of economic analysis and financial NPV (FNPV) and financial IRR (FIRR) in the case of financial evaluation.

22.   However, the perspectives and objectives of the two analyses differ. Financial evaluation is carried out from the perspective of the project, and considers incremental cash flows (both revenues and costs) generated by the project. The purpose of financial evaluation is to assess the ability of the project to generate adequate incremental cash flows to recover its financial costs (capital and recurrent costs) without external support. On the other hand, economic analysis is carried out from the perspective of the entire economy, and it assesses overall impact of a project on the welfare of all the citizens of the country concerned. The purpose of project economic analysis is to assess whether a project is economically viable for the country.

23.   The different perspectives and objectives between the two analyses mean that there are major differences in the specification and valuation of project benefits and costs. Financial evaluation is based on market prices that are actually paid or received by a project, and it focuses on financial values of project costs and benefits. Economic analysis uses economic prices, also called "shadow prices," and it focuses on economic values of project costs and benefits. Deviations of financial values from economic values of project costs and benefits arise from two major sources: price distortions and nonmarketed impacts.

Price distortions

24.   Price distortions are often created by government interventions such as taxes, subsidies, and price controls, or by imperfect competition (monopoly):

(i)   Taxes and subsidies are transfer payments, which affect the distribution of financial costs and benefits between the project entity and other stakeholders, such as the government and households, but do not reduce or increase the amount of resources available for the country as a whole;

(ii)   Price controls are imposed by the government or regulatory bodies and often involve setting prices below their market-clearing levels, making them only partially reflect the true value of the goods or services to consumers and resulting in unsatisfied demand;

(iii)   Monopolistic pricing is where producers take advantage of their dominant market position to set prices above the long-run cost of supply.

Nonmarketed outputs, inputs, and impacts

25.   Some public sector projects produce outputs that are not transacted through markets. The typical examples are public schools or public health facilities; non-toll roads; and environmental protection. In other cases, project impacts are incompletely marketed such as water and sanitation. Many projects, although they produce outputs that are transacted through markets, generate externalities that affect the society at large but are not internalized—that is, not reflected in market prices of their outputs and inputs. Externalities can be negative, such as pollution from a coal-fired power plant; or positive, such as reduced incidences of disease outbreaks due to a water and sanitation project.

26.   For these types of projects, the lack of market prices for their outputs, inputs, or impacts means alternative measures of economic benefits and costs are needed. For example, economic benefits of investment in public schools can be measured by education's contribution to productivity growth; benefits of road improvements can be measured by reduced vehicle operating cost and time savings; and benefits

of environmental protection can be measured by savings in health expenditure or avoided output losses.

27.   Economic prices reflect the economic value of goods and services and provide important guidance on the choice of public sector projects. Conceptually, economic price can be defined as the gain (or loss) in social welfare associated with consuming an additional unit of a commodity. Social welfare can be measured by the consumption of commodities or services available to a society, whether these are sold or not sold in a market. Thus, economic benefits of project output are their contribution to increasing the consumption available to society. Economic costs of project inputs reflect consumption sacrificed elsewhere by diverting the resources to the project from other uses. The value of the total net change in consumption available to the society represents the net economic impact of the project.

C.   Economic Analysis and Financing Modalities

28.   ADB projects are financed under various modalities such as investment projects, sector projects, a multitranche financing facility (MFF), financial intermediation loans (FILs), sector development programs, emergency assistance loans (EALs), and results-based lending.[5] Regardless of funding modality, where tangible and measurable outputs and associated cost streams can be identified and attributed to a specific project, project economic analysis should be carried out. The analysis can be applied to the entire project, or a specific component of the project. However, the guidelines do not apply to ADB's policy-based lending that focuses on policy and institutional reforms, and the countercyclical support facility that provides budget support.[6]

Project lending

29.   Project lending is the most commonly used funding modality in ADB. It requires physical investments and produces tangible outputs such as roads, electricity, and drinking water; and services such as transport, education, and health. Typically, investment projects are narrowly focused and have a clearly defined and known scope at the time of project preparation. Economic analysis should be thorough, with in-depth due diligence across all the key areas.

---

[5]   This sections should be read in conjunction with the various sections of the ADB Operations Manual. http://www.adb.org/documents/operations-manual
[6]   For economic analysis of policy-based lending, see Bolt, R., M. Fujimura, C. Houser, F. De Guzman, F. Nixson, and J. Weiss. 2004. *Economic Analysis of Policy-Based Operations: Key Dimensions.* Manila: ADB.

Sector lending

30.   Sector projects are a form of project-related investments aimed to assist in developing a sector or subsector by financing a series of investments. A sector project could also focus on improvements in sector policies and strengthen institutional capacity. Sector lending is expected to achieve greater impact on a sector than a stand-alone project would by enabling an integrated focus on sector development plans and policies and on the adequacy of institutions to formulate and manage such plans.

31.   Unlike an investment project, the full details of a sector project's scope are not usually known at the time of project preparation, and only a handful of subprojects may have been identified. Even in cases where all the subprojects have been identified, the full range of investment costs and benefits for individual subprojects may not be known. Given this, the economic analysis of a sector project can focus on a set of representative subprojects at the project preparation stage. If the selection of subprojects is completed only during project implementation, economic considerations should form part of the selection criteria to be developed at the project preparation stage.

Multitranche financing facility

32.   The MFF is a flexible financing modality that supports a DMC's medium- to long-term investment plan in a given sector or subsector. An MFF can support multiple projects, or large stand-alone projects requiring multiple components to be implemented over a long period. Approval of MFFs is a two-stage process, with the ADB Board approving the overall MFF investment program and ADB Management approving the individual periodic financing requests.

33.   When an MFF consists of multiple projects each with multiple subprojects, it becomes similar to a sector project, in which some of the representative subprojects are known at the outset, but the entire scope is not known. In such cases, the economic analysis for individual projects can follow the approach described for the sector project, and economic considerations should form a key part of the selection criteria to ensure that subsequent projects and subprojects funded under the MFF are economically viable. Furthermore, economic analysis will need to be updated every time ADB receives a new periodic financing request to ensure that the proposed projects are economically viable.

34.   If an MFF is composed of several independent projects, the economic analysis will treat each individual project as a stand-alone investment project and

demonstrate its economic viability. In other words, each periodic financing request will include an economic analysis for the requested investment.

35.   When an MFF has a number of interlinked components of a large and complex project, the economic analysis will analyze the overall MFF as one single investment and evaluate its economic viability. In such cases, each periodic financing request will update the original analysis based on the most recent cost and benefit estimates and implementation time line.

36.   Given that an MFF may be implemented over a period of up to 10 years, the analysis should include sensitivity tests at the outset to ensure that a slippage in implementing one or more projects does not have undue effects on the MFF's viability.

Financial intermediation loans

37.   FILs are provided to one or more entities that then channel the loans to the final borrowers for eligible subprojects. FILs can be provided on a stand-alone basis, or as components of sector development programs or sector or project loans. Examples may include provision of a credit line to one or more commercial banks that then lend to end borrowers for setting up or expanding small and medium-sized enterprises. For FILs, in addition to the rationale, demand analysis, and sustainability considerations, a thorough analysis is needed to assess the financial performance of participating financial institutions and their capacity to carry out due diligence to ensure the loans will be in compliance with ADB policies. In some cases where FILs are used to finance large infrastructure investments and the projects to be financed are well defined, economic analysis of representative projects should demonstrate that such investment will be economically viable. When representative projects cannot be identified, project selection criteria should include economic considerations.

Sector development program

38.   A sector development program is a hybrid modality, which includes both investment (investment project or sector project) and policy-based (program) components. The integrated approach combining investments and reforms helps meet a sector's needs in a comprehensive and integrated manner. An example could be a sector development program for agriculture, in which the investment component focuses on rural infrastructure investments (for example, irrigation or rural roads) and the policy-based component focuses on policy impediments to growth in agricultural productivity. Given that it has distinct investment and policy-based components, economic analysis for these components should follow the approach that is appropriate for each particular modality.

Emergency assistance loans

39.   ADB provides EALs to its DMCs to help rebuild high-priority physical assets and restore economic, social, and governance activities after emergencies. EALs, however, are not meant to provide relief or support comprehensive reconstruction activities. Given that EALs are prepared in response to an emergency situation and usually under a tight time frame, it is typically not possible to complete all the required due diligence during the preparatory stage. In the aftermath of a disaster-related emergency, it typically takes some time and effort before the extent of damage and needs can be assessed and the individual subprojects can be fully conceptualized and designed. In such cases, the EAL typically outlines the types of activities it will support and identifies the criteria for selecting subprojects during the implementation phase. As in the case of sector projects, the selection criteria need to incorporate economic considerations to ensure that the individual subprojects will be economically viable.

Results-based lending

40.   Results-based lending is to assist DMCs in designing and implementing government-owned sector programs. In general, ADB finances only a portion of a much larger program. Given this and that financing is not earmarked for any specific activities within the program, in many cases it is not possible to do a standard cost–benefit analysis and, instead, a review of the results-based lending should focus mainly on the rationale for the program, its expected economic impact, and its sustainability. However, when the projects to be financed by ADB under the program are well-defined and when specific components can be identified, standard economic analysis could be applied to demonstrate the economic viability of the projects.

D.   Design and Monitoring Framework

41.   Investment projects generally have a diverse set of effects, and project economic analysis provides a systematic framework to identify, quantify, value, and compare the economic costs and benefits of a project. It summarizes a variety of disparate effects over time into a common monetary measure, ENPV or EIRR. ADB's development mandate requires that this measure be complemented by checklists of other project impacts, for example, social or environmental, and these can be specified in a DMF.

42.   The DMF is a tool used by ADB to improve the design and implementation of projects and it should be applied in conjunction with economic analysis. The DMF sets out the links between the long-term strategic priority for a project (the impact) and the goal needed to be met in the medium term to achieve this (the outcome).

When the medium-term goal is established, the outputs which the project must target will be identified, along with the inputs and related activities necessary to achieve these.

43.　　The DMF is thus a tool to be used in identifying the parameters likely to be critical to project success, whose valuation will be important for the economic analysis. In turn, the economic analysis and the DMF should be consistent, so that outcome targets in the DMF (typically assessed at 12–24 months after project completion) correspond to the figures used to estimate benefits during the comparable year in the economic analysis. Similarly, the key risk factors identified in the DMF should be incorporated in the project economic analysis when sensitivity or risk analysis is undertaken. ADB's updated design and monitoring framework guidelines provide a DMF template and detailed requirements.[7]

III. IDENTIFICATION OF PROJECT BENEFITS AND COSTS

A.　　With and Without Project Scenarios, Constant Prices, and Project Life

44.　　There are four broad steps in project economic analysis:

(i)　　Identify gross project benefits and costs;
(ii)　　Quantify and value the benefits and costs, initially in market or financial prices;
(iii)　　Adjust the costs and benefits to reflect their economic values; and
(iv)　　Compare gross economic benefits with economic costs.

45.　　To identify project benefits and costs, the without project scenario should be compared with the with project scenario. The without project situation may not necessarily be the status quo. What matters is what would happen in the absence of the project. In comparing project alternatives, the same without project scenario should be used throughout.

46.　　In economic analysis, project benefits and costs are measured in constant prices of a base year and, therefore, the effect of general inflation is eliminated. However, relative price changes for important project cost or benefit items should be allowed in instances where there is sufficient information to do this. Different

---

[7]　For DMF, see ADB. 2016. *Guidelines for Preparing the Design and Monitoring Framework.* Manila. https://www.adb.org/sites/default/files/institutional-document/32509/guidelines-preparing-dmf.pdf

items may experience different rates of inflation because of, for example, changes in productivity, technology, or demand. In the event an item, which is a significant benefit or cost for a project, is expected to experience a differential rate of inflation, a relative price adjustment should be made for the years in which relative price changes occur. Appendix 2 illustrates the use of constant prices in economic analysis.

47. Project benefits and costs should be identified to cover both the implementation period of major investments and operating years known as the project operating life. The number of operating years to be included in the analysis is usually determined by the technical life of a project, which is the number of years of normal operation before a project is fully worn out. In cases where the economic life of the project can be estimated and there is evidence that this will be significantly shorter than the technical life, the economic life should be used. The economic life is defined as the number of years before the annual economic cost of operations begins to exceed annual economic benefits.

48. When economic life is shorter than technical life, some assets will not be fully worn out at the end of the project period. The remaining value of these assets—their terminal or residual value—is entered as a negative investment cost (that is a benefit) at the end of the project. This can be calculated approximately as the proportion of the technical life still remaining for a particular subcategory of assets, multiplied by the constant price value of the concerned assets, or as a resale value when the concerned assets can be sold.

49. A project statement provides a useful framework to present annual cost and benefit flows for each year of project implementation and operation and is therefore recommended. Appendix 3 illustrates the construction of a project statement.

B.   Identification of Benefits

50. In identifying project benefits, two distinctions are particularly important. The first is whether the benefits are derived from incremental outputs or from nonincremental outputs—in general, the approach to benefit valuation differs between these two types of outputs.[8] The second distinction is whether project outputs are sold in markets, and whether there are market prices that can be used as the starting point to value project benefits. These two distinctions and the basis for benefit valuation under various situations are illustrated in Figure 2.

---

[8]   As shown in Appendix 4, when project outputs are marketed, market is competitive, and there are no price distortions, the distinction between incremental and nonincremental outputs is not necessary and both can be valued using market prices as a starting point. However, in many cases, outputs produced by ADB projects are not marketed, or although marketed, the market is not competitive and prices are distorted. In these circumstances, the distinction between incremental and nonincremental outputs is important.

Figure 2: Identifying Project Benefits

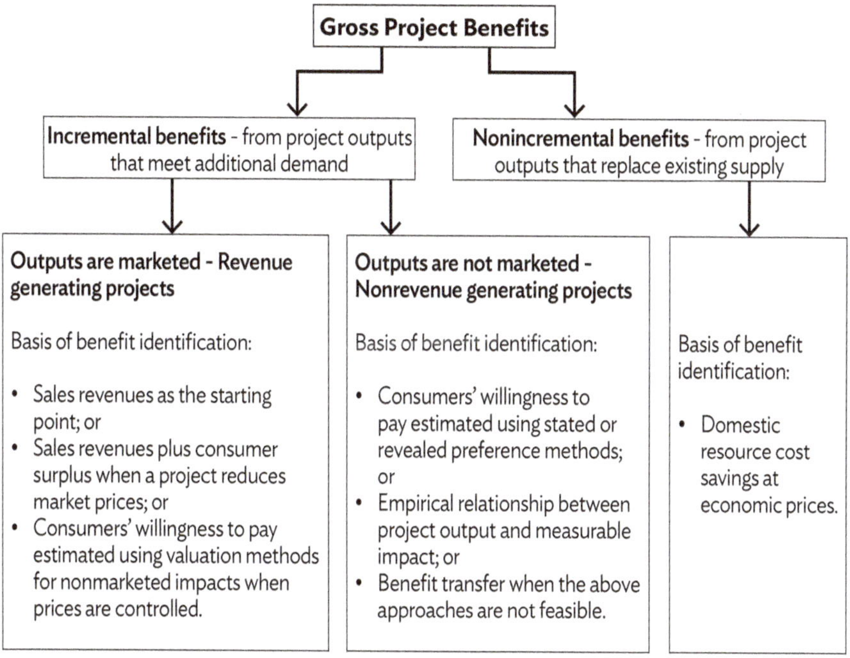

Source: ADB Economic Research and Regional Cooperation Department.

Benefits of incremental marketed outputs

51.   Incremental outputs are project outputs that expand supply to meet additional demand—as opposed to replacing existing supplies. Whether a particular project will produce incremental or nonincremental outputs often depends on project specific circumstances. In many cases, a project may produce some incremental outputs and some nonincremental outputs. Part of the process of project economic analysis is to identify these outputs based on available information such as demand forecasts, user surveys, secondary source estimates of price elasticities of demand and supply for the goods or services concerned, or insights from comparable projects implemented in the past.

52.   When project outputs are incremental, the basis for project benefit valuation is consumers' willingness to pay. The starting point for estimating willingness to pay is usually sales revenues, which are to be adjusted to eliminate various price distortions. This is the case for all internationally traded goods and services, such as agricultural products, electricity for export, and transport services serving foreign customers, as well as services that are not internationally traded, but sold in domestic markets such as electricity, water, and some transport services.

53.   A large project may lower the market price of its output, especially in the case of nontraded goods or services. This will bring additional gains to consumers because of the difference between what consumers are willing to pay and what they will actually pay with the project. These gains, called the consumer surplus, should be included as an economic benefit in addition to what the consumers actually pay. In such cases, consumers' willingness to pay as a measure of gross benefits of incremental project output is the sum of sales revenues and consumer surplus. In the absence of price controls and distortions, consumer surplus can be approximated by half of the difference between the market prices with and without the project multiplied by the quantity of incremental output (Appendix 4). Where markets are regulated with price controls, valuation methods that are often applied in valuing nonmarketed impacts can be used to establish willingness to pay (see discussion below).

Benefits of incremental nonmarketed outputs

54.   When project outputs are incremental but not sold in markets and there are no market prices, proxy measures of project benefit should be estimated. Gross economic benefits of the project can be measured by consumers' willingness to pay, and the willingness to pay can be estimated using either stated preference methods, such as contingent valuation and choice modeling; or revealed preference methods, such as hedonic pricing and averting expenditure. These valuation methods have wide applications in estimating values of willingness to pay for a range of nonmarketed goods and services such as pollution abatement, preservation of historical sites, the scenic value of the natural environment, and new vaccines for public health.

55.   When such valuation studies are not feasible, gross project benefits may be approximated by measurable impacts, such as increased incomes, improved productivity, time savings, or better health outcomes, on the basis of their empirical relationships with project outputs, similar to a dose–response relation. Such relationships may be estimated from cross-sectional data. For example, the impact of rural roads on village incomes can be estimated using a sample of villages with and without access to rural roads; the impacts of clean water and sanitation on population health outcomes can be estimated using a sample of townships with and without access to clean water and sanitation.

56.   When project economic benefits are estimated based on measurable impacts, it is important to avoid double counting. Examples of double counting include the inclusion of land value increases in addition to direct estimates of health benefits from a water and sanitation project; in addition to higher crop yields from an environmental protection project; or in addition to estimates of transport benefits from a road improvement project. In all these cases, as identifying land

value changes represents an alternative way of capturing benefits, land value increases should not be added to the other estimates.

57.   In cases where detailed valuation studies using either preference-based or measurable impact–based methods are not feasible, the benefit transfer approach can be followed when there are existing valuation studies for similar projects in similar conditions (physical, demographic, and economic). This can involve transferring unit values of benefits, or a benefit function linking an impact variable, such as willingness to pay, with appropriate explanatory variables. The benefit function transfer allows differences between the current project and reference projects from which the benefit function is being transferred to be controlled for. In using the benefit transfer approach, a meta-analysis of the existing studies applicable to the project is usually recommended, and the current project and the reference projects from which benefit values are being transferred should be comparable.

58.   Appendix 5 gives more detail on the various methods for valuing nonmarketed impacts.

59.   For some social sector (such as education and health) projects, quantification of the monetary value of project benefits is sometimes difficult. In such cases, cost-effectiveness analysis should be applied. Outside the social sectors, it is also possible that some benefits, particularly external effects, may not be quantifiable. Where it is important, but difficult to establish monetary values for such effects, they should be identified and a qualitative discussion be provided.

Benefits of nonincremental outputs

60.   Nonincremental outputs are project outputs that substitute for existing production. Where outputs of a project are nonincremental, their benefits can be measured by savings of domestic resource costs from replacing the existing production. For example, a new hydropower plant may in part substitute for the electricity generation of an existing coal-fired power plant. The benefits of the electricity generated by the hydropower plant that replaces that of the coal-fired power plant are measured by cost savings from the reduced production or closure of the coal-fired plant. Such cost savings should be valued at economic prices.

Demand analysis as the basis for benefit estimation

61.   Sound demand analysis is central to benefit estimation. How demand analysis is best carried out is likely to vary between types of projects and by the time and resources available. Broadly, there are three approaches—surveys, trend extrapolation, and forecasting models. Household surveys are a ready source of

data, which can be used to establish the baseline and existing patterns of use. For example, electricity or water consumption in villages where these services are already connected can give an indication of future use in similar or comparable villages about to receive the service. In addition, if designed properly, surveys can establish how much users are willing to pay for such services, and this information can be used to establish consumption levels at the projected tariffs.

62.   A relatively crude approach is to extrapolate past trends into the future, either on the basis of the average growth over a relatively short number of years, or where a longer time period is available by fitting a time trend in a regression model. Another version of this approach uses projections of growth of gross domestic product or household income based either on recent past trends or official projections of long-term growth and combines this information with the relationship between income and demand for the good or service. This relationship is the income elasticity of demand defined as the percentage change in demand over the percentage change in income, holding other variables affecting demand constant.

63.   A more robust approach is the use of regression-based models, which relate demand to a set of explanatory variables. The explanatory variables may include income, price of the product or service, prices of substitute products and services, and other sector or product specific factors. Such models can normally be estimated from a time series of past data. Once a model is estimated, forecast values of the explanatory variables can be used to derive demand projections from the model. Multiple regression analysis is an improvement over simple extrapolation, but in some sectors it may be necessary to go further and forecast demand allowing for the expansion plans of other enterprises or production units in a wider sector model. In the power sector, for example, least-cost expansion plans can be drawn up based on sector specific modeling.

C.   Identification of Costs

64.   The incremental and nonincremental distinction is also relevant for inputs and in identifying costs. In the incremental case, where supply is expanded to meet project demand, the value of inputs is their marginal cost, since this reflects the resources that must be committed to meet additional project demand. In the nonincremental case, where supply is fixed in the short term and project demand draws the input away from other users, the cost of the input will be determined by what other users are willing to pay for it, as this reflects its opportunity cost in terms of additional consumption that the input can produce elsewhere. In addition to this distinction, different types of costs need to be distinguished.

Capital cost and contingencies

65.   Investment costs will vary between types of project, but normally including land, buildings, machinery and equipment, and various aspects of construction and installation. These costs should be shown in the project statement against the years in which the activity takes place. For most projects, they are phased across more than 1 year. Maintenance or replacement expenditure on capital assets during a project's life should be shown in years during which the expenditure is made. Most capital cost estimates contain an element of contingency.

66.   Contingency allowances, which are determined by engineering and financial considerations, also have implications for economic appraisal. When estimating project costs for financial planning purposes, both physical and price contingencies are included. Since economic returns are measured in constant prices, general price contingencies should be excluded from the economic cost of the project. Physical contingencies represent the monetary value of additional real resources that may be required beyond the base cost to complete the project, and should be treated as part of the economic cost. Hence, for project economic analysis, it is appropriate to include the physical contingency allowance, but not the price contingency.

Working capital

67.   Working capital is the cash, accounts receivables and payables, and physical stocks of goods (both as outputs and inputs) that a project requires for its continued operations. Of these items, only physical stocks of goods are treated as a cost in project economic analysis. Accounts receivable is the value of credit advanced to the purchasers of project output and accounts payable is the value of credit received from suppliers of inputs to the project. The difference between the two is the net credit position. The net credit position is treated as a transfer between the project and other enterprises and not a real resource cost in economic terms. Similarly, the cash held by the project is not included as an economic cost on the assumption that cash is not in short supply and that the holding of extra cash by one project does not deprive another of cash needed to finance transactions. Appendix 6 illustrates the treatment of working capital.

Depreciation and interest during construction

68.   In cases where the financial statements of project executing and/or implementing agencies include provisions for depreciation and amortization, this accounting recognition of depreciation and amortization is not considered in

economic analysis to avoid double counting of capital costs. This cost already appears in the years in which the capital expenditure is made and replacement expenditure is included as needed during the project's life. However, it should be noted that the depreciation calculated for tax purposes reduces a project's profit tax liability and therefore influences the distribution analysis. Interest charges accrued during project construction are similarly not included in capital cost in project economic analysis, since the cost of committing capital to the project is covered by discounting and their inclusion would also constitute double counting.

Transfer payments

69.   Some of the items included in the financial costs of a project are not economic costs, as they do not increase or decrease the availability of real resources to the rest of the economy. These items will, however, affect the distribution of financial costs and benefits between the project entity and other entities, and among project beneficiaries. They are thus referred to as transfer payments, as they transfer command over resources from one party to another without reducing or increasing the amount of resources available for the economy as a whole.

70.   Taxes, duties, and subsidies are examples of items that, in some circumstances, may be considered transfer payments. They can affect the incomes of the government and of the payers or recipients simultaneously, but in opposite and identical amounts, thus canceling out in an economic analysis. However, there are circumstances when the tax elements should be included in the price of an input or output. The economic cost of a nonincremental input diverted to a project from other users should include the tax element, since the tax paid by other users is part of their willingness to pay. Similarly, the economic value of incremental outputs will include any tax element imposed on the output (such as value-added tax), which is included in the market price and is therefore part of consumers' willingness to pay.

External costs

71.   Some projects impose costs on others, which are not reflected in their financial statements, examples being air and water pollutions, carbon emissions, and other environmental hazards. As far as possible, all identifiable external costs should be considered in project economic analysis as part of project costs. This means, for example, that a project (such as a road or power plant) that adds to pollution should have an extra stream of cost given by the volume of pollution valued in economic prices.

Sunk cost

72.   A project may require the use of facilities already in existence. If such facilities have no alternative use, their costs are sunk costs and should not be included in the project cost. A typical example is when an additional investment is needed to complete an existing project under implementation. Economic analysis for deciding whether the additional investment is viable should include benefits related to the existing project if these benefits would not be achieved without the additional investment, but exclude the asset costs already incurred if the assets of the existing project have no alternative use, that is, they are a sunk cost.

System cost

73.   If a project is part of a larger system, the expected benefits may not accrue unless some other investments are made in the system. A typical example is a power generation project, the benefits of which rely also on investments in transmission and distribution. In this situation, the project boundary must include the total system investment required to achieve the project and system benefits. If the total system investment is viable, then the project can also be considered viable. For such projects, a system approach is often needed for economic analysis, that is, both system costs and benefits are identified and valued.

IV. ECONOMIC VALUATION OF BENEFITS AND COSTS

74.   Economic valuation of project benefits and costs involves converting their financial values into economic values, also known as "shadow pricing." This conversion requires economic prices of project outputs and inputs to be estimated. Economic prices reflect values of goods, services, and other project effects on the national economy. The basis for estimating economic prices differs between internationally traded and nontraded goods and services, between project outputs and inputs, and between incremental and nonincremental outputs and inputs. These differences are summarized in Table 1. Appendix 7 gives examples of deriving economic prices.

A.   Economic Prices of Traded Goods and Services

75.   For traded project outputs and inputs, the basis for deriving economic prices is world market prices, because international trade represents an alternative to domestic production. In the case of traded outputs, if the project impact is

Table 1: Economic Prices of Project Outputs and Inputs

	Traded or Nontraded	Incremental or Nonincremental	Basis of Deriving Economic Prices
Output	Traded	Incremental	World price – export price
		Nonincremental	World price – import price
	Nontraded	Incremental	Domestic market price or willingness to pay
		Nonincremental	Savings in domestic resource cost
Input	Traded	Incremental	World price – import price
		Nonincremental	World price – export price
	Nontraded	Incremental	Domestic resource cost
		Nonincremental	Domestic market price or willingness to pay

Source: ADB Economic Research and Regional Cooperation Department.

incremental, that is, the outputs are to meet additional demand, the export price can be used to derive the economic price; if the project impact is nonincremental, that is, the outputs are to substitute for imports, the import price can be used to derive the economic price.

76.   In the case of traded inputs, if they are incremental, that is, obtained through additional imports, the import price should be used to derive the economic price. If they are nonincremental, that is, obtained through diversion from other existing uses, the export price can be used to derive the economic price, as they could otherwise be exported.

77.   Both export and import prices are prices at the border or port of a country and need to be adjusted for the transport and logistics costs of moving outputs from the project to the border and inputs from the border to the project. These adjusted world prices are sometimes termed border parity prices (BPPs). For imports, a BPP is the cost, insurance, and freight (CIF) price paid for imports at the port or, for landlocked countries, at the railhead or trucking point, plus the cost of transport, distribution, and handling (TDH) in moving the goods to the project or to the point of consumption. For exports, a BPP is the free on board (FOB) price received for exports at the port, railhead, or trucking point, minus the TDH cost.

78.   Project outputs that substitute for imports should be adjusted for the difference between the TDH cost of moving the outputs from the project site to the domestic market and that of moving the outputs from the border to the domestic market. If the former is smaller, the difference is a net benefit created by the project and should be added to the CIF value of the project outputs that substitute for imports. Where the TDH cost is higher for moving the outputs from the project site to the domestic market, the difference should be subtracted from the project output's CIF price.

79.   Project inputs that reduce exports should also be adjusted by the difference between the TDH cost of the inputs being used by the project and that of the inputs being exported. If the TDH cost is greater for being exported, the difference is a net saving and should be subtracted from the FOB value of the exportable inputs. Similarly, where the TDH cost is greater for being used by the project, this is an additional cost and should be added to the FOB value. Table 2 summarizes all these adjustments.

Table 2: Border Parity Prices

	Project Impact	Border Price	Required Adjustments
Outputs	Exports	FOB price	less TDH from project to border
	Substituting imports	CIF price	plus TDH from border to consumption point less TDH from project to consumption point
Inputs	Imports	CIF price	plus TDH from border to project
	Reducing exports	FOB price	less TDH from production point to border plus TDH from production point to project

CIF = cost, insurance, and freight; FOB = free on board; TDH = transport, distribution, and handling costs.
Source: ADB Economic Research and Regional Cooperation Department.

80.   Where world prices for project outputs and inputs fluctuate, annual average prices should be used. World prices may be subject to long-term relative movements and, where these can be estimated, they should be allowed for. Also, there should be an adjustment for any quality difference between the foreign reference products and actual project outputs and inputs. In most cases, world prices will not be affected by a single new project and, for practical purposes, the assumption can be made that a project will influence world prices and will buy and sell outputs and inputs at given world prices.[9]

81.   All tariffs on imports and subsidies on exports are omitted from economic prices as these are transfer payments, and not resource costs. Tariffs and subsidies on foreign trade affect the domestic market prices of traded goods and services and influence the economic valuation of foreign exchange, but they do not influence the economic prices of specific goods and services.

---

[9]   However, where a project produces a high proportion of the world output, it could lower the world price and this effect (on the new and existing outputs) should be taken into account. Similarly, where a project creates additional demand for an input that is large relative to world supply, it could increase the world price, and this effect (on the new and existing inputs) should be taken into account. In both cases, price elasticity estimates are needed to estimate the effects of a project on world prices.

B.   Economic Prices of Nontraded Goods and Services

82.   ADB lends predominantly, although not exclusively, in areas where the project outputs are nontraded, such as power, water supply, and transport services. The domestic market price of nontraded outputs—which are incremental and thus add to consumption and are sold in a relatively competitive market—presents consumers' willingness to pay and can be used to value output provided that there is no evidence of excess demand and rationing at this price and that the project will not have a significant downward impact on the market price. The domestic price should be inclusive of any indirect tax (which is part of willingness to pay) and exclusive of any subsidy on the sale of output (which represents a transfer from the government to the producer). When a project leads to a reduction in the market price, willingness to pay per unit of output should be used for driving economic price, and this is the sum of the market price and consumer surplus (see para. 53 and Appendix 4).

83.   Some projects, particularly for public utilities, produce nontraded outputs that are incremental and sold in markets with price controls and excess demand and, hence, market prices or user charges are not appropriate as the basis for economic valuation. Some other projects, such as those relating to environmental protection, produce incremental outputs that are nonmarketed and, hence, there are no market prices. Under these circumstances, willingness to pay or project benefit per unit of output can be estimated using methods for valuing nonmarketed impacts such as contingent valuation, choice modeling, hedonic pricing, or averting expenditure (paras. 54–58 and Appendix 5). When undertaking a new valuation study is not feasible and there are existing studies for similar projects in similar contexts, the benefit transfer approach can be followed provided that the existing studies are considered comparable.

84.   When nontraded outputs replace the existing production, they are nonincremental. These nonincremental outputs should be valued at the marginal economic cost saved per unit for the displaced production, which is exclusive of any indirect tax (which is a transfer from producers to the government) and inclusive of any production subsidy (which is to compensate producers to recover full resource cost).

85.   Nontraded goods and services used as project inputs, where they are incremental—a project results in expanded production of these inputs, should be valued at their marginal economic costs of supply, exclusive of any indirect tax and inclusive of any production subsidy. Marginal economic cost will differ between situations where spare capacity exists and only variable operating costs will increase, and in situations where there is no existing spare capacity and the marginal production

cost includes a capital cost element. In either case, the traded component of the marginal cost must be valued at world prices as discussed earlier.

86.   Where a nontraded input is nonincremental, the valuation of the input should be based on an estimate of what the average user is willing to pay for retaining supplies of the input. In practice, it will be acceptable to take this as the domestic market price unless there is excess demand at that market price.

C.   The Economic Price of Labor

87.   The economic price of labor, also termed the shadow wage rate (SWR), should capture the cost to the economy of employing an additional worker on a project. The economic price of labor may be different from the actual wage paid to the worker because of unemployment and underemployment caused by the existence of surplus labor or wage controls by the government. In general, with some simplification, three categories of labor can be distinguished with different implications for the economic cost of labor: (i) skilled labor that is in scarce supply; (ii) unskilled and semiskilled labor that is in surplus supply and is openly unemployed; and (iii) unskilled and semiskilled labor that is underemployed.

88.   Skilled labor of category (i) consists of workers who would be able to find alternative employment quickly and where supply is fixed in the short term. This generally includes those with specialist skills and in vocational, technical, or managerial roles. For skilled labor that is scarce, the actual wage rate paid by the project inclusive of benefits can be taken as its economic cost. In the relatively rare case where wage controls and barriers to labor mobility mean the economic cost is greater than the wage actually paid, an upward adjustment to the actual wage paid can be made.

89.   Skilled foreign labor can be considered as in scarce supply and its economic price will be the cost of its local consumption at economic prices, plus any remittances from the country of employment to the country of origin, plus the cost per worker of any additional facilities, such as health or education services, that have to be provided for foreign workers and are not included in project costs. For practical purposes, it can normally be assumed that all of these costs will be captured in the wages (inclusive of benefits) paid.

90.   Labor of category (ii) consists of workers who are in surplus supply and have to spend a long search time between jobs with some never finding full-time work. For workers employed by a project who were openly unemployed, the economic price will be determined by the monetary compensation they will require to take on work, termed the reservation wage (usually based on income provided by their family and/or any state unemployment benefits).

91. Category (iii) is likely to be more relevant for unskilled or semiskilled labor in low and lower middle income developing member countries (DMCs) with limited state welfare systems and large informal sectors. In category (iii), the shadow wage will be determined by the output forgone in informal sector activities in either rural or urban areas as a result of workers' employment on a project plus, where migration from rural to urban areas is involved, any additional costs of social infrastructure provision (such as housing, health, and education services) not borne by the project itself. Where the output forgone can be identified precisely (such as a crop like rice or cotton), an estimate can be made of the value of production lost using the economic price of the individual output.

92. A proxy measure often used for the opportunity cost of rural unskilled labor is the daily wage for rural casual labor on the assumption that rural labor markets for unskilled casual employment are sufficiently competitive so that the actual wage rate reflects daily productivity. Daily rates can be reexpressed in annual terms, allowing for seasonal open unemployment, and used as a measure of opportunity cost to compare with the full time annual project wage. However, when there is minimum wage legislation, the actual wage rate could exceed the opportunity cost.

93. The SWR for different categories of labor can be expressed in relation to the actual wage rate paid by the project of the same category of labor to form the shadow wage rate factor (SWRF), so SWRF = SWR/w, where w is the actual wage. Where labor is an important component of project costs or workers are a key beneficiary group, a detailed analysis of the local labor market should be undertaken to estimate the local opportunity cost of project labor, which will give a project specific SWRF. Where labor is a relatively small element in project cost or is not a major project beneficiary, there will be no need to do a detailed calculation and an approximate national estimate of the SWRF will be sufficient.

94. For scarce or skilled labor, the national SWRF can normally be taken to be 1.0. For surplus labor where detailed information on the likely shadow wage is unavailable, the impact of using different national SWRFs can be tested in sensitivity analysis. Appendix 8 illustrates estimation of the SWR and the SWRF.

D. The Economic Prices of Land and Natural Resources

95. All projects involve use of some land. Even where it has no financial cost, its economic value should be estimated and included in the calculation of project economic viability. As for other resources, in principle, the economic value of land should reflect its opportunity cost and determined by what the land would have been used for without the project. Where the land market is relatively competitive, the purchase or lease price provides a relatively simple proxy for economic value or

opportunity cost of land. But where there is a strong speculative element in the land market, as is often the case in fast growing areas, land market sale or rental prices can be a poor guide, and the underlying economic value of land or its opportunity cost should be estimated directly.

96. Estimating the opportunity cost of land directly will differ from case to case. In broad terms, a distinction can be made between changing land use in (i) rural areas, where agricultural production will be lost; (ii) city areas, where a range of services and activities may be displaced; and (iii) special development zones, where the production structure is changing rapidly and land may have been otherwise largely undeveloped. For new projects in rural areas, the opportunity cost of the land will be the net agricultural output foregone, measured at economic prices. A similar approach can be used for city-edge land, where agricultural uses are displaced by infrastructure, industrial, or housing projects.

97. In estimating opportunity cost, the existing land use should be assessed and a land suitability analysis carried out for the most likely without project alternative. Commonly, a specific product or small number of products will be selected to represent the lost net output from the land. Estimates based on per unit of land can be made and then projected onto the total land area. Where it is observed that agricultural techniques or cropping patterns are changing, an annual adjustment to the lost output per unit of land can be made to reflect changing productivity without the project. The net benefits per harvest from the selected products must be adjusted by the cropping intensity to give the annual loss of net output for the land area.

98. Where land is a relatively small part of project cost, purchase or lease prices provide a simple proxy for the economic value of land. Where land is an important component of costs at the prevailing market valuation, a detailed assessment should be carried out to determine how far there is a speculative element in this price.

99. Many ADB projects have a resettlement component. The full costs associated with the resettlement, including the alternative use of the land involved, should be included in the economic analysis. Appendix 9 illustrates the economic pricing of land and resettlement.

100. Many projects involve the exploitation of a nonrenewable natural resource such as oil, natural gas, or mineral deposits. The economic cost of using these natural resources should be included in the economic analysis. Because these national resources cannot be replenished and, when depleted, they must be replaced by imports or domestic substitutes, the opportunity cost of such a resource includes the cost of the substitutes when the resource is exhausted, which is termed the depletion premium. The depletion premium depends on the economic price of the resource

in the future and the proportion of the total reserves exploited during each year. It is added to the economic cost of exploitation to arrive at the full economic cost of using the nonrenewable resource. If the resource will not be exploited to exhaustion, the terminal value of the land at the end of the project should include the economic value of any remaining reserves that are not depleted. Appendix 10 discusses the depletion premium in more detail.

E.   Shadow Exchange Rate: Bringing Economic Prices to a Common Base

101.   If the above principles are followed in estimating economic benefits and costs, traded outputs and inputs will be valued at world prices, while nontraded ones will be valued at domestic prices (or willingness to pay). World prices in a foreign currency (usually the US dollar) will have to be converted into a local currency or vice versa using an exchange rate. Because of trade protection and other factors such as transaction costs, domestic and world prices for comparable goods when expressed in the same currency using the official exchange rate can be different, with the former higher than the latter. The difference represents the extent to which domestic consumers are willing to pay above the direct foreign exchange cost of the traded goods and services. Bringing economic prices to the same currency and same price level so that project benefits and costs can be aggregated and compared requires using the shadow exchange rate.

102.   The shadow exchange rate (SER), also termed the economic price of foreign exchange, can be defined as the ratio of the value of all traded goods and services in an economy at domestic prices in local currency to the value of all traded goods and services in an economy at world prices in foreign currency, expressed in the number of local currency units per unit of foreign currency, usually the US dollar. In economies where foreign currency is scarce, the SER is greater than the official exchange rate, indicating that domestic consumers place a higher value on imported and exported goods and services than is given by their world prices at the official exchange rate. Even where the official exchange rate is market determined, it can differ from the SER because of factors such as trade protection, transaction costs, and capital flows.

103.   The ratio of the SER to official exchange rate is the shadow exchange rate factor (SERF), which with trade protection is usually greater than 1. Multiplying output and input values measured at world prices and converted at the official exchange rate by the SERF, while leaving those at domestic prices unadjusted, brings the former to a common base of measurement with the latter, which is in the currency of the

borrowing country at its domestic price level. This is called using the domestic price numeraire (see Appendix 11 for an illustrative example).[10]

104.   The SER and resulting SERF are macroeconomic parameters and their estimation should be done from time to time on a country basis as part of a macroeconomic assessment of individual DMCs. Estimation of the SER can be based on an adjustment to the prevailing official exchange rate for the overall level of protection in an economy. In addition, where the real exchange rate at the time of project preparation deviates from the underlying or equilibrium real exchange rate over the life of the project, this should also be allowed for. In practice, there is often an implicit assumption that the current real exchange rate is not misaligned with the underlying economic fundamentals and that the difference between domestic and world prices for internationally traded goods is determined solely by taxes and subsidies on foreign trade; but this may not be true under some circumstances. Appendix 12 gives an illustrative example of estimating the SER.

105.   When the level of trade protection is low and there is no evidence of a real exchange rate misalignment, the analysis can be simplified by setting the SER equal to the official exchange rate and, hence, the SERF and the standard conversion factor are in unity, so no exchange rate adjustment is required. However, even with low protection, it will be important to gauge how far an adjustment of the real exchange rate will take place over the life of a project. Evidence on this will be major shifts in the commodity terms of trade, large changes in capital inflows, and productivity growth differentials with trade partners. How far these trends need to be taken into account is a macroeconomic issue and advice needs to be sought from the appropriate country economists for the country concerned.

F.   Conversion Factors

106.   Individual project items can be valued at their individual economic prices. However, for ease of calculation, economic values of project outputs and inputs can also be derived from their financial values using conversion factors (CFs). A CF is a ratio between the economic value and financial value of a project output or input. Provided this ratio is assumed constant over a project's life, values at financial prices can be multiplied by this ratio to give the corresponding economic values. Some CFs

---

[10]   An alternative approach to bringing economic prices to a common base is to multiply output and input values measured at domestic prices by the standard conversion factor, which is simply the inverse of SERF, while leaving values at world prices converted at the official exchange rate unadjusted. This is called using the world price numeraire. The two approaches—using the domestic or world price numeraire—will yield the same EIRR. Use of the domestic price numeraire is more intuitive and has the advantage of using the same price level as the financial analysis, so the distributional effect of a project can be traced more easily.

will be project or product specific, while national conversion factors (like the SERF) are country specific and should be updated from time to time to reflect a country's changing circumstances and, once established, should be applied to all the projects of a country consistently.

107.   CFs can be calculated at different levels for

(i)   specific items, which are important to a project as the main outputs and inputs;
(ii)   project specific labor, where labor is an important cost element;
(iii)   nontraded inputs, which occur in nearly all projects, for example, transport, water, and power where the supply of these nontraded inputs is expanded to meet project demand; and
(iv)   the economy as a whole, such as SERF and a national SWRF.

108.   The approach of applying individual CFs to project items separately can sometimes involve unnecessary detail. With the assumption that both CFs and the share of different cost and benefit components remain constant over the life of a project, a simpler approach is to decompose the financial price data on all project benefits and costs into a small number of resource categories, which can then be revalued by the respective CFs. This has the advantage of allowing the sensitivity of assumptions about economic prices to be tested easily.[11]

109.   Table 3 groups project cost and benefits into a small number of categories and shows their respective conversion factors and how they can be derived, using the domestic price numeraire. Nontraded items not valued at willingness to pay are grouped together as costs. In a more detailed analysis, however, these nontraded items may be further decomposed into their traded, labor, and transfer components, and appropriate conversion factors applied accordingly. Appendix 13 illustrates the use of CFs in more detail.

Table 3. Cost and Benefit Categories and Conversion Factors Using Domestic Price Numeraire

Category	Financial Values to Be Adjusted	Conversion Factors to Be Applied
Traded	All traded costs/benefits at world prices that are converted at the official exchange rate	SERF

continued on next page

---

[11]   This approach is illustrated in Chapters 7, 8, and 9 of ADB. 2013. *Cost–Benefit Analysis for Development: A Practical Guide*. Manila.

Table 3. continued

Category	Financial Values to Be Adjusted	Conversion Factors to Be Applied
Nontraded	Incremental benefits and nonincremental costs	1.0 or, when there is consumer surplus, ratio of willingness to pay per unit to the financial price
	Nonincremental benefits and incremental costs	1.0
Scarce labor	Wages of skilled workers	1.0
Surplus labor	Wages of underemployed or unskilled workers	SWRF
Transfers[a]	Taxes and subsidies	0

SERF = shadow exchange rate factor, SWRF = shadow wage rate factor.
[a] Indirect tax on output sales should be included as part of willingness to pay for nontraded output.
Source: ADB Economic Research and Regional Cooperation Department.

V. BENEFIT VALUATION IN DIFFERENT SECTORS

110.   Unless otherwise indicated, benefit valuation as discussed below refers to gross benefit of a project, rather than its net benefit that is the difference between gross benefit and cost. While the general principles of benefit valuation—distinguishing between nonincremental benefits that are measured at cost savings and incremental benefits that are measured at market prices (where there is no consumer surplus) or willingness to pay—apply to all sectors, detailed applications differ among sectors.

A.   Transport

111.   Transport projects, covering road, rail, ports, and airports, provide direct benefits to users such as access to markets and services, lower travel time and cost, comfort, and safety. Transport projects bring benefits to the existing (normal) traffic, which includes that of using the existing route in the absence of the project, that diverted from other routes or modes, and the traffic on other routes and modes benefiting from traffic diversion as a result of the project. Benefits for normal traffic are nonincremental and can be valued in cost savings measured at economic prices. Transport projects may also generate new traffic and, hence, incremental benefits, which should be valued at willingness to pay.

Road projects

112.   Road projects usually involve constructing, improving, or rehabilitating intercity highways, innercity urban roads, or rural feeder roads. Nonincremental

benefits are based on cost savings, typically including vehicle operating cost (VOC) savings and time cost savings, plus accident cost savings, and reduction in environmental impacts.

113.   VOC savings vary by vehicle type (such as cars, trucks, buses) and are influenced by road characteristics (such as surface roughness, width, curvature), vehicle characteristics (such as speed, weight, age), and costs (such as prices of vehicle and fuel, and maintenance costs for parts, materials, and labor). For road improvements, VOC savings are typically calculated using the Highway Development and Management Model.[12] For traffic diverted from other routes or modes, VOC savings can be estimated by comparing the VOC of the road project under consideration with that of the other routes or modes. When the traffic diversion reduces costs for existing users on other routes or modes from where the diversion takes place, such cost savings should also be included as a benefit.

114.   Time cost savings can arise from reduction in travel distance, or in congestion, or from faster road speeds, and can benefit both passengers and cargo in transit. For passengers, when measuring benefits from time savings, the analysis should separate work from leisure time, with the value of work time saved usually based on the relevant hourly wage rate, and that for leisure time approximated by a proportion of the hourly wage. For cargo, shorter trip time means the earlier delivery of goods. This benefit can be estimated based on the reduction in working capital as a result of the earlier delivery of goods and opportunity cost of capital, which can be approximated by the minimum required EIRR. Where perishable goods are involved, the time savings may create an additional benefit in avoided spoilage cost.

115.   Accident cost savings include avoided medical expenses; avoided damage to vehicles, properties, and road structure; avoided income loss due to injuries; and avoided deaths. These can be estimated using data on accident related medical expenses, replacement cost of assets, and income loss per accident, as well as estimates of the statistical value of life. When country specific data are not available, data from other countries of similar economic conditions and at a comparable income level may be used.

116.   Road projects also generate environmental impacts, and these should be considered in economic analysis. For clean transport projects, for example, reduction in air pollution, in carbon dioxide (CO_2) emissions, or in other environmental effects associated with normal (existing) traffic could be major sources of benefit. Air pollution or CO_2 emissions can also be reduced as a result of reduced congestion. Benefits from reduction in air pollution can be approximated by the cost of air

---

[12]   See Highway Development and Management Model (HDM-4) at http:// hdmglobal.com>

pollution in avoided health expenditure and loss of productive time. Quantification and valuation of benefits from CO_2 emission reductions or reductions in CO_2 equivalents for other greenhouse gases are discussed further below.

117.   When a road project generates new traffic, it brings incremental benefits, which should be measured at willingness to pay. The willingness to pay for each unit of generated traffic can be approximated at the average of the perceived user costs with and without the project including tolls. When a project involves modal shifts, which is often the case in the urban context, the without project scenario will be sufficiently different from the with project case to require direct estimation of willingness to pay through a valuation study using methods such as contingent valuation (Appendix 5). When a road project generates additional traffic, the resulting negative environmental impacts should be included as costs or negative benefits.

118.   For rural feeder roads, the application of the Highway Development and Management Model may not be appropriate as there will typically be virtually no motorized traffic without the project. In this case, an alternative approach is to estimate net income gains for rural households and firms, where appropriate, created by the improved access allowed by a new project. This requires assessing the impact of road access on net incomes in the catchment area, controlling for as many other factors as possible that are likely to affect income.

Other transport projects

119.   Rail projects typically aim to improve railway services and network infrastructure. Nonincremental benefits are reductions in user costs for existing passengers, freight shipments, and operators. Where a project causes a diversion of traffic from roads to rail, the cost savings will accrue not just to those users diverted to rail, but also to those who continue to use the road network as a result of lower congestion there. Cost savings can in principle occur through a wide range of sources, including more efficient use of fuel and materials; reduction in crew, passenger, and cargo time; more efficient utilization of rolling stock; reduction in working capital; and reduction in accidents and in pollution and CO_2 emissions. Incremental benefits are the value placed on additional travel generated by the project.

120.   Airport transport projects usually involve construction, upgrading, or rehabilitation of airport infrastructure and associated facilities to increase the capacity to handle higher traffic. Investment projects in airport infrastructure can be divided into those devoted to processing aircrafts (named airside) and to those processing passengers (named landside). Nonincremental benefits refer to cost reductions for existing users (passengers, cargoes, and operators) resulting from lower travel, access and waiting time; improvements in service reliability

and predictability; and reduction in operating costs. Cost savings will also impact on traffic diverted from other modes like rail or road as a result of improved air services. Airport transport projects will generate incremental benefits when they generate additional passenger and freight traffic as a result of cost reduction and improvements in frequency and services. These should be estimated following the approaches discussed.

121.   Port projects include construction of new ports or upgrading existing ones to increase passenger and cargo handling capacity as well as to improve operational efficiency. Where they ease congestion, reduce ship waiting time, or lower anchorage and berth and cargo-handling cost for existing traffic, cost savings per unit of cargo and/or passenger handled will define nonincremental benefits. Incremental benefits are the additional traffic handled by a port due to the project, and can be measured at willingness to pay.

122.   When transport projects serve both domestic and foreign users, such as airports, seaports, and cross-border roads or railways, they provide traded services. For these projects, benefit valuation must distinguish between benefits accruing to foreign users (foreign airlines, shipping companies, and cargo and passengers) and those to domestic users. Benefits from serving foreign users can be measured by actual user charges, received in foreign currencies, and adjusted by a SERF as appropriate.

B.   Power

123.   Most power projects are part of a system network. Power generation projects add capacity to the system to expand supply, to increase efficiency thereby reducing generation costs, and/or to improve the reliability of electricity supply. Power transmission projects link generation capacity with a distribution system, and distribution projects link the evacuated power from the grid to final users.

124.   In most cases, benefits of power projects are realized only when power is consumed by final users—they create no value independent of other parts of the power supply network. Therefore, in appraising power expansion programs, it is common to follow a system approach, by identifying both benefits and costs of generation, transmission, and distribution lines associated with the extra investments that are required in the overall power system to give a net benefit figure.

Generation projects

125.   Generation projects often increase output by expanding capacity or improve efficiency by displacing or rehabilitating old facilities that have lower efficiency and

higher operation and maintenance costs, or both. When output remains unchanged with and without a project, benefits are entirely nonincremental and can be measured by cost savings on fuel, equipment, and labor from the displacement or rehabilitation. For renewable projects that displace the existing fossil fuel generation facilities, nonincremental benefits include not only cost savings, but also those related to reduction in CO_2 emissions and other net environmental benefits.

126.   When a generation project increases capacity, the increased output can consist of two components. One is supplied to new users to replace their existing energy sources such as kerosene- or diesel-powered generators. The benefits from this are nonincremental and can be valued at cost savings. The other is to increase consumption by the existing and new users. The incremental consumption should be valued at willingness to pay. When there is no government price control on electricity tariffs, the willingness to pay for incremental outputs can be approximated by the average of without and with project tariffs for the existing consumers and, for the new consumers, the average of the unit cost of the without project energy source and with project tariff. If this approach is judged misleading, a valuation study using methods such as contingent valuation can be applied to estimate willingness to pay (Appendix 5).

127.   The benefit of incremental consumption from a generation project will also depend on the availability of surplus capacity in transmission and distribution. If surplus capacity is not available to allow incremental consumption, extra investment in transmission and distribution will be required. In such cases, a system approach should be applied by combining the generation project with the transmission and distribution components so that their investment and operating costs are added to the project cost to derive net benefits.

128.   Improvements in service reliability in power supply are largely characterized by a reduction in outage costs that are often associated with supply interruptions (blackouts), frequency and voltage reductions (brownouts), or sharp fluctuations in frequency and voltage. When the power project has a distinct component of system reliability improvement, willingness to pay for this improved service can be either estimated directly or approximated by avoided outage costs. In the latter case, improvements in reliability are valued by estimating domestic resource cost savings, such as avoided costs of backup generators or reduced income losses, as a result of the project.

Transmission and distribution projects

129.   Transmission and distribution projects reduce line losses, both technical and commercial, expand network capacity, and extend access to electricity to areas where

no electricity is available. When the network capacity remains the same with and without a project, the project benefits are entirely nonincremental and can be valued at resource cost savings such as reduced line losses resulting from the project. When a project expands network capacity or extends access, the increases in capacity or coverage generate nonincremental as well as incremental benefits. Nonincremental benefits occur when users switch from their existing energy sources, such as kerosene- or diesel-powered generators to new sources of supply made available by the project, and these can be valued at resource cost savings. Incremental benefits are associated with increased electricity consumption by both new and existing customers and can be valued at willingness to pay.

130.   The benefit of incremental consumption from a transmission (or distribution) project will also depend on the availability of surplus generation and distribution (or transmission) capacity. If surplus capacities are not available for incremental consumption, extra investment would be required. In such cases, again a system approach should be applied by combining the transmission, distribution, and generation components in the appraisal, so that the extra cost elsewhere in the system is added to the project cost to give net benefits. Benefits from improvements in reliability of service are also relevant for transmission and distribution projects.

Rural electrification

131.   Supply expansion carried out in a rural area with no prior access to electricity—distribution grid extension or decentralized power supply—is often referred to as a rural electrification project. Where a rural electrification project connects previously unconnected customers to the grid or provides more efficient energy sources (such as renewables), the project generates both nonincremental and incremental benefits. The nonincremental benefits arise from the existing energy sources being replaced by the new sources associated with the project, and can be valued at cost savings. Incremental benefits arise from increased electricity consumption and should be valued at willingness to pay. This can be approximated by the average of the unit cost of the without project alternative energy source, such as kerosene lighting, and the with project tariff, or estimated through a valuation study using methods such as contingent valuation (Appendix 5).

C.   Water

132.   Water supply projects offer either improved services to households already connected to the main system or provide connections to households not yet served who, without the project, would otherwise rely on less satisfactory sources of supply such as wells, standpipes, or water vendors. In the case of the already connected

households, the project may improve reliability or quality or expand supply, while in the case of those not connected, the project may offer a qualitatively different supply. Water supply projects may also increase supply by reducing technical losses, i.e., water produced but lost to leakages. Projects that improve water quality are likely to generate health benefits.

133.   For previously unconnected households, output that substitutes for existing supplies is nonincremental and output that meets additional consumption is incremental. Benefits from nonincremental output can be approximated by the savings of resource costs associated with the existing supplies such as charges for water from vendors (where applicable) plus time spent on collecting water and fuel spent in boiling water. Time savings can be valued at a proportion of the casual daily unskilled wage rate in the project locality adjusted by the SWRF. Benefits from incremental output should be measured by willingness to pay. Willingness to pay can be approximated by the average of per unit user costs with and without project, or estimated through a valuation study using methods such as contingent valuation[13] (Appendix 5), or through benefits transfer (Appendix 14).

134.   For previously connected households, only incremental benefits are to be included. When a project leads to significantly improved services—in reliability, quality, and supply, the improved services can be considered incremental for both previously connected and unconnected households, so all water demand is treated as incremental and measured by willingness to pay, to be estimated following one of the approaches described above as appropriate.

135.   A water supply project may generate benefits by reducing technical losses resulting from avoided leakages. When a water supply project introduces a metering system, it can also lead to more efficient use of water resources. These benefits can be treated as incremental as they will add to consumption.

136.   Health benefits can be expected to accrue from the provision of clean water to replace lower-quality supplies. These are additional benefits when valuing nonincremental output. They can be estimated in terms of avoided public and private medical costs and gains in income and productivity due to lower incidence of illness. For incremental output, the measure of willingness to pay used should in principle have already considered positive health benefits from improved water supply and, hence, no separate valuation of health benefits is needed.

---

[13]   Examples of applying the contingent valuation method to estimate willingness to pay for water supply and sanitation projects are provided in ADB. 2013. *Cost–Benefit Analysis for Development: A Practical Guide*. Manila.

D.   Urban Development

137.   Urban development projects are multisector and often include components of water supply and sanitation, wastewater treatment, solid waste management, urban rehabilitation, transport and environmental improvements, and housing. Where subcomponents of an urban project can be treated as discrete activities, so that benefits and costs of one subcomponent are not dependent on the implementation of other subcomponents, project economic analysis should be undertaken for each subcomponent. However, where subcomponents are interrelated and benefits and costs of one subcomponent are dependent on the implementation of the other subcomponents, these subcomponents should be appraised as an integrated unit, that is, following a system approach.

138.   Urban development projects are typically accompanied by increases in land value, which are sometimes taken as proxy measures of economic benefits from an integrated project. Because many factors affect land prices, and there is also often a strong speculative element in price increases, this approach could be misleading. As much as possible, efforts should be made to identify and value individual benefits other than land prices.

Wastewater treatment and solid waste management

139.   Benefits from these types of projects can usually be considered fully incremental as they add a new improved service. As an incremental service, benefits can be valued at willingness to pay, which can be estimated through valuation studies using methods, such as contingent valuation (Appendix 5), or following a benefit transfer approach where appropriate (Appendix 14). Benefits of improved sanitation and solid waste management services can also be approximated by estimates of health-related cost savings from avoided health damage through surveys. If the "without project" scenario entailed significant time and resources cleaning latrines and affected areas, these avoided costs can also be included as benefits.

140.   Wastewater treatment and solid waste management projects often lead to increases in land value. Estimating the expected change in land value provides an approximate way of estimating project benefits, provided that the land value change can be attributed entirely to the project. This can be done by comparing the land value of the project area with that of a similar control area with better sanitation, using techniques such as hedonic pricing (Appendix 5), to control for other factors that affect land value. When expected increases in land value are included as project benefits to avoid double counting, expected health-related cost savings should not be included. Since land values in urban areas can rise rapidly, in practice it is often

difficult to attribute causation to a single factor, so that this approach should be applied with extreme care.

141.   Solid waste management projects may involve separation of waste and composting. If any separated waste is reused, its resale value and that of the organic fertilizer generated by waste processing can be added to the benefits, provided its value is not already included in any willingness to pay estimate.

Urban transport

142.   Urban transport projects often include road improvements, new road construction, and mass transit systems covering rail, tram, or bus links. The principles of benefit valuation discussed above for the transport sector remain valid. Normal traffic and traffic diverted from one mode to another (for example, from road to metro) will be valued at the cost savings arising from a new project. Additional traffic generated can be valued at willingness to pay, which can be approximated by the average of unit user travel costs with and without the project, or estimated through a valuation study applying methods such as contingent valuation, or following the benefit transfer approach.

143.   A key objective of urban transport subprojects is often to reduce congestion, particularly on roads, which can create significant external benefits in time savings on other routes and modes and reductions in pollution and CO_2 emissions. These external effects should be valued and incorporated in the economic analysis.

144.   Estimation of cost savings and traffic diversion in an urban context can be highly complex, as metro or ring road projects often create significant shifts across transport modes. In such cases, the analysis should be done as part of a master planning exercise. If a transport subproject is a component of a wider urban development program, it may be possible to draw on data from a master plan to assess the extent of traffic diversion and generation.

Urban rehabilitation

145.   Urban rehabilitation projects usually include subcomponents, such as improving or restoring a riverbank, lighting, park and recreation areas, and urban sites, with the overall objective of making the city more livable and attracting more domestic and foreign tourists. When the specific amenities will overwhelmingly benefit local communities, their benefits can be measured by willingness to pay, which can be estimated using valuation methods for nonmarketed impacts such as contingent valuation, choice modeling, or hedonic pricing.

146.   If the objective of an urban rehabilitation project is to develop the tourism industry, its benefits can also be estimated in terms of the expected net increase in local incomes resulting from incremental tourist expenditures. This would require estimating expected increases in the number of tourists and their length of stay as a result of the project, tourists' daily expenditures with and without the project, and the income multiple of tourist expenditures. These can be obtained through surveys or following the benefit transfer approach. In such cases, it is important to make a distinction between foreign tourists and domestic ones. An increase in the number of domestic visitors in the project area may imply a reduction in other areas within the economy. This substitution effect needs to be deducted when estimating the net increase in the number of domestic tourists in the project area.[14]

147.   River improvements, covering for example the cleaning of polluted and silted rivers, civil works to straighten and stabilize riverbanks, and environmental improvements, such as tree planting and construction of riverside paths, are sometimes linked with solid waste management and wastewater treatment. In such cases, river improvements can be considered as a part of the linked subprojects, and separate benefit valuation of the river component may not be required. When river improvements are not linked with water treatment or waste disposal, it will be difficult to attribute any direct health benefits to river subprojects and they may need to be appraised on a cost-effectiveness basis to ensure that the least-cost technical option is selected.

Housing

148.   Slum clearance and the provision of new housing can be an important component of some urban projects. These subprojects can be treated as providing a new service and thus can be seen as wholly incremental. Benefit valuation can be based on market rental rates for properties of comparable size and located in a comparable area, regardless of whether a market rent is actually charged for the new houses or whether property sale to beneficiaries is on commercial terms. A residual value for the property can be set at the end of the project's life as a proportion of the market value in constant prices at the time of construction with this value discounted back to the present.

E.   Agriculture and Natural Resources Management

149.   Agriculture projects usually involve one or more of the following— constructing or rehabilitating irrigation systems; introducing new farming

---

[14]   See ADB. 2007. *Tourism for Pro-Poor and Sustainable Growth: Economic Analysis of Tourism Projects*. *ERD Technical Note*. No. 20. Manila. https://www.adb.org/sites/default/files/publication/29863/tn-20-tourism-pro-poor.pdf

technologies, including crop varieties; providing agriculture extension services such as building storage facilities and market information and training; supporting research and development in agriculture; and increasing livestock and fishery production. Natural resources projects include interventions aimed at improving the management of land or water resources such as forests, wetlands, watersheds, and aquatic environments including fisheries.

Agriculture

150. The principal benefits of agriculture sector projects consist of increased output resulting from improved productivity or enhanced yields and reduced unit production costs or losses. Benefit valuation of a typical agriculture sector project (such as irrigation) follows the following steps. The first is to estimate crop outputs with and without the project in the project area for each individual crop on the basis of representative data. The difference in outputs between with and without project cases can be a result of changes in yield per hectare, in output loss during harvesting, in cropping pattern and intensity, in cultivated areas, or a combination of these changes. It is important that with and without project comparisons capture differences solely resulting from the project.

151. The second step is to decide the economic price for each crop. Most agricultural outputs are tradable with prices given to individual countries; thus, world prices can be used as the basis for benefit valuation for most agriculture sector projects. These are export prices in the case of incremental outputs— when the outputs are to meet new demand—and import prices in the case of nonincremental outputs—when the outputs are to substitute for imports. In both cases, the economic price is measured at the farm gate level, by adjusting the world price for transport, distribution, and handling costs from the border or from the port to the farm.

152. Some projects may lead to higher output of nontraded crops produced for a local market. Where the change in supply resulting from the project is sufficiently large to reduce the price in that market, there will be effects on both consumers and producers, since consumption will increase (representing incremental output) and output from nonproject suppliers may fall (representing nonincremental output) because of a lower price. The net effect of these changes in willingness to pay and cost savings can be estimated with assumed values for price elasticity of demand and supply for the crops concerned. The sum of these effects will determine project benefits.

Natural resources management

153.   Natural resources management projects usually aim to increase output or the sustainability of marketed products through implementation of scientific management methods or improved governance and/or management arrangements for collectively owned resources. To the extent that such projects are intended to improve productivity, they can be analyzed using similar methods to agricultural productivity enhancement and irrigation projects.

154.   Natural resources management projects often involve efforts to conserve use and non-use values from uncultivated ecosystems. For example, improved forestry may be intended to protect biodiversity, avert greenhouse gas emissions, and prevent erosion. Coastal management projects may intend to help conserve coral reefs and fish populations for biodiversity, tourism, and fisheries sustainability purposes. Watershed management interventions may aim to improve water quality and reduce erosion. These benefits mostly arise through nonmarketed effects, and can be estimated through a valuation study using methods, such as contingent valuation, choice modeling, or hedonic pricing, or, where these are not feasible, following the benefit transfer approach.

F.   Environmental Protection and Conservation

155.   Environmental projects refer to those that have environmental protection and conservation as their major source of benefits. Typical examples include projects for pollution control, protection of the ecosystem, flood control, and control of deforestation. An environmental project generates nonincremental benefits when the project replaces the existing protection at the same level. Nonincremental benefits can be estimated as domestic resource cost savings from shifting from the existing protection to the new protection provided by the project. Domestic resource cost savings can be measured by the difference between costs of providing the same level of protection without the project and those with the project, including damage aversion expenditure incurred by the government, households, and firms.

156.   When a project provides a higher level of protection and conservation, it will generate incremental benefits. Incremental benefits can be measured in avoided environmental damage because of the project and estimated in a number of ways. Where the environmental damage affects marketed goods (such as income losses caused by soil erosion, deforestation, or flooding), benefits from avoided damage can be estimated based on the technical or ecological relationship between environmental damage and its impact on outputs of the marketed goods, similar to a dose–response relation, with the change in outputs valued at economic prices.

An increasingly important category of risk reduction intervention concerns "climate proofing," or ancillary project investments to reduce risks to new investment projects posed by future climate change.[15] The benefits of such interventions can also be measured in damage avoided.

157.   Where incremental benefits involve nonmarketed impacts, valuation studies can be carried out using preference-based methods (such as contingent valuation, choice modeling, hedonic pricing, or averting expenditure) to assess willingness to pay for the value put on environmental quality by the respondents. Such methods can be employed, for example, to determine the amenity value of species or landmarks and to determine willingness to pay for better access to clean water and improved sanitation.

158.   Primary research on environmental impact by applying one of these methods will be justified for dedicated environmental protection projects or where there are major unmitigated environmental effects. However, when there are constraints on time, data, and budget for applying these methods, the benefit transfer approach of taking values estimated in other similar contexts for similar projects may also be used when considered as appropriate. When using the benefit transfer approach, the most relevant values estimated in other contexts need to be identified and modified as necessary for the conditions of the specific project.

159.   Appendix 14 gives examples of applying the benefit transfer approach. There is now a large literature on environmental valuation, which can provide the starting point for benefit transfer estimates.[16]

G.   Climate Change and Greenhouse Gas Emissions

160.   A special and important case for environmental valuation is estimating the value placed on greenhouse gas (GHG) emissions, either as benefits where a project reduces emissions, or costs where it increases them. Contributions of an individual project to emissions or mission reductions can cover a number of GHGs including methane (CH_4) and nitrous oxide (N_2O), although CO_2 is likely to be the most important for valuation purposes. The impact of changes in other gases can be treated as CO_2 equivalent.

---

[15]   These are discussed in ADB. 2015. *Economic Analysis of Climate Proofing Investment Projects.* Manila.

[16]   The Environmental Valuation Reference Inventory website (www.evri.ca), for example, has created a detailed database of environmental valuation studies. Information is grouped initially by continent, study topic (for example, air, water, or land), and methodology (market prices, revealed preference, stated preference). Each entry contains a summary of the original study and thus permits identification of suitable comparison work.

161.   Some projects may reduce emissions from nonincremental outputs, but increase emissions from incremental outputs. For instance, road improvement can reduce congestion that helps to reduce emissions from the normal traffic, but can also generate new traffic that increases emissions. The net change in emissions as a result of a project should be identified and valued, which can be done through a with and without project comparison. Emission accounting should be carried out as part of the environmental impact assessment normally based on technical relationships between different emissions and a measure of project activity (such as emissions per kilowatt-hour of electricity or per liter of fuel used).

162.   Reduction of GHG emissions can be treated as a global gain and their increase as a global loss. Although individual countries may be affected in only a limited way from global impacts, given ADB's policy on climate change, it is appropriate to include global climate-related gains or losses as part of economic benefits and costs generated by a project. For the purposes of project economic analysis, the EIRR and/or ENPV with and without considering global impacts of GHG emissions should both be reported, and the one with the global impacts should be used as the basis for making investment decisions. Cost-effectiveness analysis should also incorporate the social cost of GHG emissions.

163.   In valuing GHG emissions, it is important to use a standard value, also called global social cost of carbon, across all projects. A review of the empirical estimates of the global social cost of carbon reported by the International Panel on Climate Change[17] suggests a unit value of \$36.30 per ton of CO_2 or its equivalent in 2016 prices for 2016 emissions, to be increased by 2% annually in real terms to allow for the potential of increasing marginal damage of global warming over time. This unit value can be used to estimate the benefit in damage avoided for projects that reduce emissions and the cost in damage created for projects that increase emissions. The unit value may be revised in the future as more and new estimates of global warming damage become available.

H.   Education

164.   Education projects typically involve improving primary, secondary, and tertiary education, as well as technical and vocational education and training (TVET). They can include upgrading or expanding school buildings, designing or modifying the curriculum and teaching materials, developing education information management systems, and strengthening other monitoring, evaluation, and management systems. TVET projects may include the improvement of a job-matching system.

---

[17]   See Intergovernmental Panel on Climate Change. *Fifth Assessment Report* (AR5). https://www.ipcc.ch/report/ar5/

165.   Education projects can generate a wide range of economic and social benefits. Economic benefits can include resource cost savings through system improvement, higher employment, and increased labor productivity and earning opportunities. Intangible social benefits can include a healthier lifestyle, greater gender equity and social mobility, and more tolerant cultural attitudes. However, these social benefits often cannot be adequately measured and valued at project level.

166.   Where adequate benefit valuation is not possible, cost-effectiveness analysis, comparing a measure of educational impact with project costs, should be applied, which can be supplemented by a multi-criteria analysis. Some education projects will have objectives that lend themselves to a full project economic analysis. For example, when the objective of a project is to increase effectiveness of service delivery (such as upgrading of education information management systems and management capacity improvements) or to reduce costs without increasing capacity (such as reorganization), the benefits will be nonincremental and can be measured in resource cost savings resulting from the project.

167.   Projects that expand access to education produce incremental benefits. In some cases, such as projects related to TVET, incremental benefits may be measured by the employment and the earnings potential of students who graduate through the program, as compared with the employment and earnings with a lower education or training level in the without project case. The impact of additional years of education on earnings may be estimated from survey data using statistical models. However, such results are often subject to a high level of uncertainty, and the sensitivity of project results to their assumptions needs to be tested.

168.   When a full economic analysis is carried out for an education project, it is important to distinguish public benefits from private benefits. Private net benefits are post-tax higher earnings minus private education costs, such as fees and travel, and lost earnings while at school beyond the school leaving age. Public net benefits, which are the focus of economic analysis, are higher earnings minus the full cost of education, including both additional private costs (but excluding any fees as these are a transfer from households to the project or the government) and costs of investing in and operating the project concerned.

I.   Health

169.   Health projects involve improving the coverage and quality of health care provision, including upgrading health facilities; providing health equipment and personnel training; and strengthening health information management, evaluation, and monitoring systems. Adequate benefit valuation in health is not always feasible because of the complexity of valuing the diverse set of health improvements.

Therefore, in many cases cost-effectiveness analysis should be used for health projects, along with examining other factors that are often considered under a multi-criteria analysis.

170.   Cost-effectiveness analysis for health projects requires estimating a measure of health impact and comparing this with the project costs of achieving this impact.[18] A satisfactory measure of health impact from an intervention must combine mortality and morbidity effects, through lower fatalities and less illness, across different patients, and weigh these in some way. The disability adjusted life years (DALY) measure is the one commonly used in development projects, and discounted cost per DALY saved is the most common approach to cost-effectiveness for health projects. If a project has very high costs per DALY by international or national standards, a justification will need to be given for these high costs, if the project is to be accepted.

171.   Some health projects, such as those for improving health system efficiency or increasing the productivity of the working population, will have objectives that lend themselves to a full project economic analysis. Projects that increase the effectiveness of service delivery, for example, by upgrading the health information system or reorganizing hospitals, will generate nonincremental benefits when the same number of patients and beneficiaries receive the same level of services but at a lower cost. These benefits can be valued at the resource costs saved. Similarly, projects that increase immunization and/or awareness for preventative disease control can be seen as generating nonincremental benefits in that they remove the need for expenditure on curative interventions to reduce illness.

J.   Regional Cooperation

172.   A regional cooperation project usually involves two or more countries and requires that the project generates benefits that would not be available to equivalent national projects located in the participating countries. When a project is part of multicountry plans, agreements, or mechanisms of regional cooperation, it can also be considered a regional cooperation project event if it involves only one country. Economic analysis of regional cooperation projects requires the calculation of the returns for both the region and individual countries. The regional economic net present value (ENPV) gives the total change in welfare for the group of participating countries, which must be equal to the sum of the national ENPVs.

173.   The principles of benefit valuation from the national case apply to regional cooperation projects. A special focus is needed to identify and value the additional

---

[18]   See Chapter 5 of ADB. 2000. *Handbook for the Economic Analysis of Health Sector Projects.* Manila.

benefits arising from regional cooperation, which will vary across sectors but are likely to be based on a variant of one or more of the following effects:

(i)   Generation of additional investment by attracting external funding, such as foreign direct investment, to at least one of the participating countries that would not be forthcoming for nationally based projects;

(ii) Facilitation of technology transfer alongside the increased foreign direct investment;

(iii) Capture of economies of scale and efficiency gains from regional specialization based on selling in a larger market;

(iv) Generation of agglomeration and network effects through the development of cross-border economic corridors; and

(v)   Creation of broad cross-border effects such as the generation of additional trade through improved transport and communications, improved environmental cooperation (such as control of floods and pollution), and greater control of transmittable disease.

174.   Where macro distortions for foreign exchange and unskilled labor are significant, national adjustments must be made to costs and benefits of traded goods and unskilled labor costs using national conversion factors. Where these factors differ between participating countries, the adjustments must be allowed for. Since several countries can be involved in a regional project, it is necessary to convert benefits and costs into a common currency (normally the US dollar).

175.   Following the calculation of the regional ENPV, including the spillover impacts listed in paragraph 173, distributional analysis of benefits across the participating countries should be carried out. Appendix 15 illustrates the application of distribution analysis for regional cooperation projects.

VI. INVESTMENT DECISIONS AND CRITERIA

A.   Discounting and Indicators of Economic Viability

176.   After identifying and valuing project benefit and cost flows accrued in different years of a project's life that normally spans over 20–30 years, the future flows should be converted to their present value (or the value of a base year) by discounting at a required economic discount rate. The discounting allows calculating aggregated indicators of economic viability of a project for making investment decisions. The most commonly used indicators to determine economic viability are economic net

present value (ENPV) and economic internal rate of return (EIRR). Other commonly used indicators are the benefit–cost ratio (BCR) and cost-effectiveness ratio (CER).

177.   The ENPV is the sum of the differences between the discounted benefit and cost flows, and can be estimated as

$$\text{ENPV} = \sum_{t=1}^{n} \frac{(B_t - C_t)}{(1 + r)^t} \qquad (1)$$

Where B_t is the gross economic benefit in year t, C_t is the sum of economic costs (including capital costs, operating maintenance costs, and negative terminal values) in year t, r is the required economic discount rate, and n is the project life.

178.   The EIRR is the discount rate at which the ENPV becomes zero, and it can be estimated from the following:

$$\sum_{t=1}^{n} \frac{B_t}{(1 + r)^t} - \sum_{t=1}^{n} \frac{C_t}{(1 + r)^t} = 0 \qquad (2)$$

Where r is the EIRR, at which, the sum of the discounted stream of economic benefits equals that of the economic costs of a project.

179.   The BCR is the ratio of the sum of the present value of the project benefits to the sum of the present value of the total project costs, and it can be estimated as

$$\text{BCR} = \sum_{t=1}^{n} \frac{B_t}{(1 + r)^t} \div \sum_{t=1}^{n} \frac{C_t}{(1 + r)^t} \qquad (3)$$

However, when project costs C_t include only fixed investment cost and exclude operation and maintenance costs, this is called the net BCR.

180.   When there is only one project option and there are no alternatives to compare with and choose from, the ENPV, the EIRR, and the BCR should yield the same result: accept the project when its ENPV calculated using a minimum required discount rate is positive, or when the EIRR is greater than the minimum required discount rate, or when the BCR calculated using the minimum required discount rate is greater than 1. However, when an investment has several alternative project options that are mutually exclusive, the ENPV, the EIRR, and the BCR may or may not yield the same result. In such cases, the use of the ENPV is recommended.[19]

---

[19]   In ranking alternatives without capital rationing, the EIRR or the BCR can be biased in favor of smaller higher yield projects. There could be other problems in using the EIRR or the BCR. For instance, there could be multiple EIRRs if project net benefit switches signs more than once. The BCR may depend on whether cost savings are counted as negative costs and deducted from costs or counted as benefits and added to benefits instead.

181.   The CER is the ratio of the present value of a project's investment and operating costs to the present value of the project output or outcome. The CER is mainly used for selecting the best project option when project benefits cannot be adequately valued and economic viability requires selecting the option with the least cost per unit of output or outcome. The CER is also useful in situations where project benefits can be valued and project alternatives have the same benefit flows so that investment decisions involve two steps, with the first step choosing the project option with the lowest CER; and the second testing whether the ENPV at the minimum required discount rate is positive or the EIRR is greater than the minimum required discount rate. The CER can be calculated as follows:

$$CER = \sum_{t=1}^{n} \frac{C_t}{(1+r)^t} \div \sum_{t=1}^{n} \frac{O_t}{(1+r)^t} \qquad (4)$$

Where O_t is output or outcome in year t, which is not in monetary terms.

B.   Project Alternatives

182.   Very often, several alternative project options achieve the same objective of an investment. The options can differ in technology, location, scale, or design, including the use of materials. For example, increasing water supply may be achieved through either augmenting capacity or improving water management. Urban traffic congestion may be addressed by improving the existing road network or building a new subway system. Regional connectivity can be enhanced by investing in waterways, roads, or railways. Project options can also involve different investment timing and include delaying a project as an alternative. Whenever possible, all mutually exclusive, technically feasible alternative options should be assessed and compared.

183.   Technology is often a critical factor for consideration in assessing project options. Some new or more advanced technologies may involve larger initial investment, but they have lower operation and maintenance costs compared with traditional ones. Therefore, it is important to look at "life cycle" costs (and benefits) when choosing technology for a project. In some cases, technology choice today may have long-term implications beyond the life of the project, for instance, when it locks an economy into a specific technology option, making it very costly to shift to an alternative technology in the future. In such cases, the choice of technology should consider factors beyond the life of the concerned project. This usually requires a sector wide assessment of the long-term technological options rather than an analysis of an individual project.

C. Investment Decisions

184. Investment projects, such as power, transport, urban development, and rural irrigation, generate economic benefits most of which can be valued, and establishing economic viability requires a full cost-benefit analysis. However, for many social sector projects, some poverty targeting projects and projects that primarily generate environment benefits, the conventional measure of economic benefits such as willingness to pay may not adequately capture their social value. For these projects, when adequate benefit valuation is difficult, economic viability of a project can be assessed based on the cost-effectiveness analysis and, when appropriate, supplemented by a multi-criteria analysis. Investment decision rules under different situations are presented in Figure 3 and discussed below.

Figure 3: Investment Decision Rules

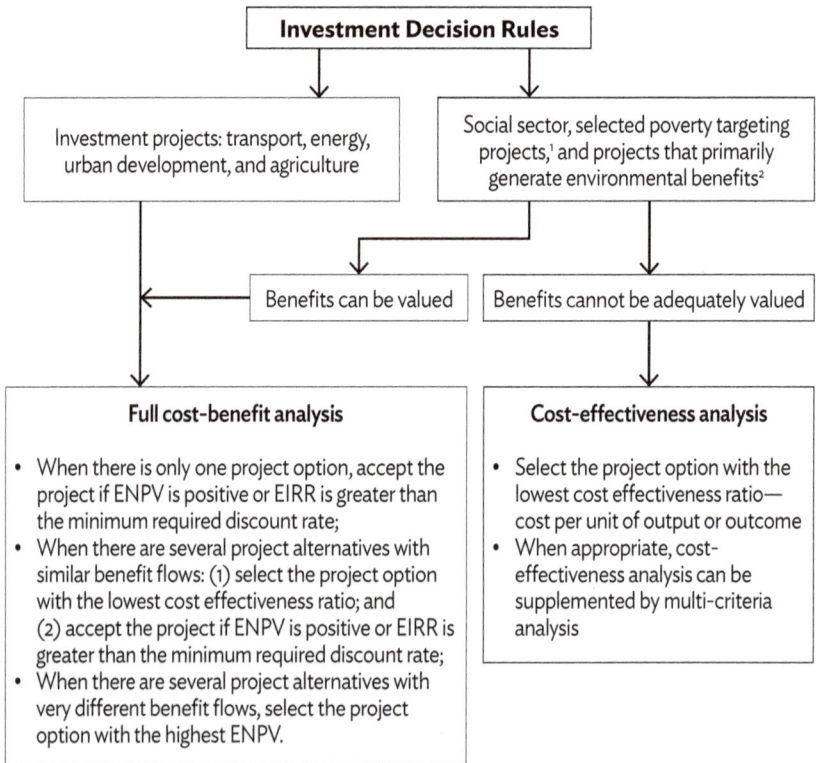

Investment Decision Rules

Investment projects: transport, energy, urban development, and agriculture

Social sector, selected poverty targeting projects,[1] and projects that primarily generate environmental benefits[2]

Benefits can be valued

Benefits cannot be adequately valued

Full cost-benefit analysis

- When there is only one project option, accept the project if ENPV is positive or EIRR is greater than the minimum required discount rate;
- When there are several project alternatives with similar benefit flows: (1) select the project option with the lowest cost effectiveness ratio; and (2) accept the project if ENPV is positive or EIRR is greater than the minimum required discount rate;
- When there are several project alternatives with very different benefit flows, select the project option with the highest ENPV.

Cost-effectiveness analysis

- Select the project option with the lowest cost effectiveness ratio— cost per unit of output or outcome
- When appropriate, cost-effectiveness analysis can be supplemented by multi-criteria analysis

EIRR = economic internal rate of return, ENPV = economic net present value.
[1] Such as rural roads and rural electrification.
[2] Such as pollution control, protection of the ecosystem, flood control, control of deforestation, and disaster risk management.
Source: ADB Economic Research and Regional Cooperation Department.

Investment decisions when benefits are valued

185.   Investment projects generate economic benefits that can usually be valued. For these projects, the ENPV, the EIRR, and the CER, when appropriate, should all be calculated. When there is only one project option, the project should be accepted if its ENPV, calculated using the minimum required discount rate, is positive, or if the EIRR is greater than the minimum required discount rate. Appendix 16 provides an illustrative example of estimating the ENPV and the EIRR for an irrigation project.

186.   When several project alternatives produce the same outputs or outcomes with the same levels and identical quality, making the investment decision can involve two steps. The first step is to select the project option with the lowest CER; and the second step is to accept the project option if its ENPV is positive, or if its EIRR is greater than the minimum required discount rate.

187.   When project alternatives produce different levels of outputs, with different quality, timing, or prices, making the investment decision requires calculating the ENPV using the minimum required discount rate for all the alternatives, and selecting the one with the highest ENPV and with investment not exceeding the budget.

188.   The timing of a project is often an important issue, since for virtually all projects there will be an option of delay. Where timing is considered, it is preferable to treat projects started at different times as separate projects and compare them using the ENPV indicator. The key is to compare ENPV values for different versions of the same project starting in different years, or equally for projects with different termination dates, but each discounted back to the same base year to give equivalent present values. The difference between the ENPV of a project and of an alternative introduced later is the value of waiting, which can be either positive or negative depending upon trends in demand and costs. In principle, the option of delaying a project should always be considered.

189.   In some project types, there may be a fixed investment budget to be allocated among a large number of small projects with insufficient funds to finance all projects with a positive ENPV. In these circumstances, project ranking can be undertaken using the net BCR. By ranking according to this indicator and accepting projects until the budget is exhausted, net benefits from the fixed investment budget will be maximized.

Investment decisions when benefits are not valued

190.   For many social sector projects (such as education and health), some poverty targeting projects (such as rural roads and rural electrification), and projects that

primarily generate environmental benefits (such as pollution control, protection of the ecosystem, flood control, and control of deforestation), where the conventional measure of economic benefits such as willingness to pay may not adequately capture their social value, economic viability of a project can be assessed based on cost-effectiveness analysis. Cost-effectiveness analysis aims to ensure that the chosen option represents the least cost among mutually exclusive, technically feasible project alternatives. Appendix 17 provides examples of cost-effectiveness analysis. When appropriate, cost-effectiveness analysis can be supplemented by a multi-criteria analysis.

191.   When all the project alternatives deliver the same level of outputs with identical quality, cost-effectiveness analysis involves estimating the present value of cost streams at a required discount rate for each of the alternative project options being examined and choosing the one with the lowest present value of costs. Sometimes, even though project alternatives produce same outputs or outcomes with an identical quality, they differ in scale. In such cases, the CER (see Equation 4) can be used to identify the least-cost option.

192.   Some projects may produce a diverse set of project outcomes, not just one—for example, educational attainments or health conditions. In such cases, a weighting scheme is needed to combine the different outcomes into a single cost-effectiveness indicator, similar to a multi-criteria analysis.

193.   Using cost-effectiveness analysis to identify the least-cost project option should also involve comparing the estimated cost-effectiveness indicator with national or international benchmarks. In making this comparison, it will be important to use the same discount rate in the project calculations as in the comparator study. A CER that is above the country average or an international benchmark need not rule out a project, however, a clear justification of why costs are high is needed, such as location of a school or clinic in a remote area. The plausibility of any such explanation will need to be assessed.

The minimum required discount rate

194.   ADB uses a discount rate of 9% as the minimum required EIRR to accept or reject a project and to choose the least-cost (or most efficient) project option for all investment projects such as transport, energy, urban development, and agriculture. This rate acts as a rationing rate to ensure efficiency in the use of its resources and as proxy for the opportunity cost of capital in individual developing member countries (DMCs). But for social sector projects, selected poverty-targeting projects (such as rural roads and rural electrification) and projects that primarily generate environmental benefits (such as pollution control, protection of the ecosystem, flood

control, control of deforestation, and disaster risk management), a lower discount rate of 6% can be applied as the minimum required EIRR.[20] When the lower rate is used, a clear rationale should be provided.

195.   ADB operates with an indicative program of lending for each country as specified in country partnership strategies and annual country operations business plans. These programs are partly determined by an assessment of absorptive capacity within the country, and what other external funds are being used. Some countries will operate under an investment budget constraint at the national or sector level. In addition, investments tend to be lumpy and not fit easily within any constraint. When a country is faced with a budget constraint, implying more investment opportunities than it can implement, an appropriate response is to raise the required discount rate above the standard 9%. Alternatively, for some economies there may be an absorptive problem, so that there may be a shortage of high return projects. In such cases, 9% may overstate the opportunity cost of capital in the economy and a lower rate may be justified.

196.   Where there is evidence that the 9% (or 6%) discount rate is not appropriate for an individual DMC, a national economic discount rate can be calculated for the country concerned. If a national economic discount rate is estimated, it should be applied to all projects in that country, rather than only selectively. Appendix 18 provides an example of estimating a national economic discount rate.

VII. SENSITIVITY AND RISK ANALYSIS

197.   Project economic analysis uses the most likely forecast values of economic benefits and costs. However, streams of benefits and costs are influenced by a wide range of factors and they may deviate from the forecasts. Sensitivity analysis aims to assess the effect of adverse changes in key variables upon the project ENPV and EIRR and the implications of these changes for the project investment decision. Risk analysis incorporates the probabilities that the key variables will deviate from their forecast values and the associated risk to the project arising when these key variables vary simultaneously. These techniques can be used to assess the implications of uncertainty for investment decisions, and should be used to inform the design of mitigating actions. Appendix 19 provides more details and examples of sensitivity and risk analyses.

---

[20] Application of a lower social discount rate to these projects can be justified on the following grounds: (i) social sector projects and poverty-targeting projects often have many unquantifiable benefits; and (ii) many environmental protection and conservation projects have very long-term impacts that justify a lower discount rate.

A.   Sensitivity Analysis

198.   Sensitivity analysis is undertaken to identify the key variables that can influence project cost and benefit streams. It involves recalculating the EIRR or the ENPV with varying values of key variables, where the variations can be independent or a combination. Sensitivity analysis usually involves the following steps:

(i)   selecting those variables to which the investment decision may be sensitive;

(ii)   determining the possible extent of variation of these variables from the base case;

(iii)   calculating the effect of different values of these variables on the project results by recalculating the project ENPV and EIRR; and

(iv)   interpreting the results and designing mitigating actions.

199.   Ex post evaluation studies and project experience may indicate both the type of variables that are uncertain and the possible extent of divergence from the base case. Key variables could include output demand, output prices, capital cost, and, in some projects, timing and delays. It is important that sensitivity analysis is not applied mechanically, such as a 10%–20% reduction in benefits or a 10%–20% rise in costs. It should focus on the specific parameters that lie behind the aggregate benefit or cost estimates, so that the true impact of a specific change can be assessed.

200.   Outputs of the sensitivity analysis generally include the following:

(i)   a table showing changes in the EIRR and the ENPV for a range of independent or correlated   changes in a number of key variables, holding everything else constant;

(ii)   a sensitivity indicator showing the ratio of the percentage change in the ENPV to the percentage change in the variable tested;

(iii)   a switching value for each key variable showing its value at which the project becomes marginal (EIRR equals 9% and ENPV at 9% equals zero); and

(iv)   the percentage difference between the switching value and the base case value for each key variable.

201.   The percentage difference between the base case value and the switching value highlights the risk level of the project in relation to key variables. The results of this analysis will then need to be interpreted in terms of the likelihood of the switching values occurring and the measures that could be taken to mitigate or reduce the

likelihood of such variations from the base case. Such measures can include long-term supply contracts for key inputs, better training for project personnel, technical assistance programs to impart operational management skills, and initiatives for institutional and policy reform.

B.   Risk Analysis

202.   Risk analysis differs from sensitivity analysis in that it estimates the expected (probability weighted) ENPV and the probability of the EIRR falling below the test rate. It involves

(i)   identifying key determinant factors or variables of project costs and benefits;

(ii)   establishing the probability distributions of these variables;

(iii)   randomly selecting values of these variables from their probability distributions;

(iv)   combining these selected values with base case values of all other variables and parameters to estimate an ENPV or an EIRR;

(v)   repeating steps (iii) and (iv) numerous times to provide a large number of ENPV and EIRR estimates and to establish their respective probability distribution; and

(vi)   estimating the probability of the weighted ENPV and EIRR, as well as the probability of the EIRR falling below the test rate.

203.   This process is called the Monte Carlo simulation. When the functional form of the probability distribution of the identified key variables for risk analysis is known, large and complete data sets are not necessary. For instance, if a particular variable is considered as following a normal distribution, the only parameters needed to establish the distribution are the mean value and its standard deviation. Establishing a triangular distribution requires only specifying "most likely," "minimum possible," and "maximum possible" values, which can be constructed based on "best guesses." Quantitative risk analysis should be considered for projects that are large relative to the borrowing DMC or that have a potentially large impact on a particular target group within the borrowing country, and for projects where there is considerable uncertainty about key aspects such as the probability of flooding.[21]

---

[21]   Details of risk analysis are in ADB. 2002. *Handbook for Integrating Risk Analysis in the Economic Analysis of Projects.* Manila.

VIII. PROJECT SUSTAINABILITY

204. Economic viability depends on the sustainability of project effects over the project's life. Hence, project economic analysis should ensure that an adequate analysis of the financial and institutional sustainability of the sponsoring agency and of the environmental sustainability of the project itself has been carried out.

A. Financial and Institutional Sustainability

205. Economic viability requires that a project is designed such that its net economic benefits will be sustained during the project's economic life. This requires demonstration of the financial and institutional sustainability of a project. To assess financial sustainability, the financial evaluation of the project and the financial analysis of the project executing and/or implementing entity must be conducted in accordance with ADB's guidelines on financial due diligence,[22] as noted in para. 17. These financial sustainability assessments will normally be drawn up as part of the financial due diligence of a project and the economic analyst should refer to these to identify any risks and shortfalls that threaten the financial sustainability of the project. The institutional capacity of project-operating entities should be assessed in all the cases.

206. In the case of a revenue generating project, its financial rate of return should be compared with its weighted average cost of capital, and the financial performance of the project implementing entities should be assessed to ensure that funds will be sufficient to operate and maintain the project.[23] For a nonrevenue project that does not generate funds to cover operating expenditures, the full fiscal impact of the project for each year of its life should be calculated and steps should be taken to ensure that the government commits adequate funds for operational purposes. Many projects will impact on the government budget, through tax revenues and concessions, and the net budget effect can also be calculated.

207. For public sector utilities, setting the appropriate level of user charges will be important. ADB policy is to seek the elimination of user subsidies where they are not justified on grounds of social priorities or where they can be replaced by more direct support such as targeted transfers. Tariff structures should be designed to ensure that users pay a tariff that reflects the cost of provision. The introduction or increase of user charges may affect the scale of the investment to be undertaken.

---

[22] See Operations Manual section G2 *Financial Management, Cost Estimates, Financial Analysis, and Financial Performance Indicators.*

[23] Financial sustainability analysis should follow ADB. 2005. *Financial Management and Analysis of Projects.* Manila.

Charges provide a form of demand management, where users react by adjusting their use to the level of charges. These effects can be estimated through the use of price elasticities of demand. Demand management of this sort is particularly important where governments lack investment and operating resources.

B.   Environmental Sustainability

208.   To address environmental concerns, projects that use natural and environmental resources should pay the full cost of use, and where they cause long term environmental damage, the projects should be required to undertake appropriate mitigation expenditure. Similarly, where projects create environmental benefits, the benefits should be valued and included in the project economic analysis. The main concerns at the project planning stage is that an appropriate environmental impact assessment has been carried out, that mitigation measures are in place, and that economic analysis has reflected fully any unmitigated environmental costs, either in monetary or nonmonetary terms.

209.   Projects can also be affected by the environment and ADB policy now requires climate-proofing issues to be considered in project design to try to minimize the negative impact of long term environmental effects on projects such as droughts, soil erosion, or floods. The economic benefits from ancillary investment designed to protect the project from potential climatic change must be assessed and compared with the cost of this protection.[24]

IX. DISTRIBUTION ANALYSIS

210.   Distribution analysis is an important component of project economic analysis. First, a project must be financially sustainable and, hence, financial incentives must be adequate for each of the main project stakeholders. Second, where the government is involved it will be important to know how far the project will add to or reduce future government financial commitments. Third, where parties from different countries are involved, it will be important to establish the distribution of net gains and costs between these countries. Finally, where projects are intended to contribute to the goal of inclusive growth, it will be important to establish how target groups are affected.

211.   As the ENPV is equivalent to a change in national income, it will affect some group within the economy. Income changes are estimated first by establishing the income flows created by the financial analysis of the project. Additional income

---

[24]   See ADB. 2015. *Economic Analysis of Climate-Proofing Investment Projects*. Manila.

changes are estimated from divergence between financial prices and economic prices. A full distribution analysis involves taking the basic data from the project economic analysis and allocating the estimated project ENPV between different groups, whether consumers, workers, investors, suppliers, and the government.

212.   A further level of disaggregation can be applied to these groups to distinguish subgroups, such as consumers or workers above and below the national poverty line or those households resettled as a result of the project. In some projects, it may also be necessary to show the effects on project lenders (where interest rate subsidies are involved), on foreign investors, and on stakeholders from different countries in the same region. A particular focus on net benefits going to the poor is relevant for many agricultural, social sectors, urban development, and some public utility projects.

213.   Distribution analysis can be used to show estimates of how the income of different groups will be affected by a project and, in some projects, it will be useful to calculate a poverty impact ratio showing the proportion of the project ENPV that goes to those below the poverty line. For such projects, even where it is not possible to estimate this ratio accurately, a statement can be provided on the number of poor users or households reached with an indication of the scale of benefits in nonmonetary terms (such as school places, kilowatt-hours of power provided or cubic meter of water made available). In general, the analysis of project impacts on the poor should be based on specific information about direct project beneficiaries, and not merely on information about the district or province in which a project is located. Obtaining information about likely beneficiaries is part of the process of project identification and design, and data collected at this stage can be used at appraisal.

214.   Project costs and benefits may have a different impact on men and women. Where a project generates substantial net benefits and extra incomes for project participants, this may be at the cost of additional work and extra effort by the participating households. The burden of additional work rarely falls equally on all members of a household. At the same time, those who benefit or control the additional financial resources may not be those who contribute most of the extra effort. For some types of projects, for example, health, education, or agricultural development projects, a distribution analysis can be undertaken on a gender basis, to identify the additional costs and benefits to women in particular.

215.   Appendix 20 provides an example of distribution analysis.

Appendix 1:
Reference Materials
on Project Economic Analysis in ADB

The following is a list of reference materials produced by ADB on project economic analysis. These are available at MyADB (internal website) and www.adb.org (external website).

1. **Guidelines and Practical Guide**
   a. Guidelines for Economic Analysis of Projects, 1987
   b. Guidelines for Economic Analysis of Projects, 1997
   c. Economic Analysis of Policy-Based Operations: Key Dimensions, 2003
   d. Cost-Benefit Analysis for Development: A Practical Guide, 2013

2. **Pamphlets**
   a. Economic Analysis of Projects: Key Questions for Consultants, 1997
   b. Key Areas of Economic Analysis of Projects: An Overview, 2004
   c. Key Areas of Economic Analysis of Investment Projects: An Overview, 2013

3. **Handbooks**
   a. Framework and Criteria for the Appraisal and Socioeconomic Justification of Education Projects, 1994
   b. Framework for the Economic and Financial Appraisal of Urban Development Sector Projects, 1994
   c. Handbook of Economic Analysis of Water Supply Projects, 1999
   d. Handbook of Economic Analysis of Health Sector Projects, 2000
   e. Handbook for Integrating Poverty Impact Assessment in the Economic Analysis of Projects, 2001
   f. Handbook for Integrating Risk Analysis in the Economic Analysis of Projects, 2002

4. **Technical Notes**
   a. Public Investment Criteria: Economic Internal Rate of Return and Equalizing Discount Rate, 1987
   b. Public Investment Criteria: Financial and Economic Internal Rates of Return, 1990

   c. Economic Analysis of Health Sector Projects: A Review of Issues, Methods, and Approaches, 1999

   d. Economic Analysis of Subregional Projects, 1999

   e. Contingency Calculations for Environmental Impacts with Unknown Monetary Values, February 2002

   f. Integrating Risk into ADB's Economic Analysis of Projects, June 2002

   g. Economic Issues in the Design and Analysis of a Wastewater Treatment Project, July 2002

   h. Measuring Willingness to Pay for Electricity, July 2002

   i. Economic Analysis of Health Projects: A Case Study in Cambodia, July 2002

   j. An Analysis and Case Study of the Role of Environmental Economics at the Asian Development Bank, September 2002

   k. Shadow Exchange Rates for Project Economic Analysis: Toward Improving Practice at the Asian Development Bank, February 2005

   l. Improving the Relevance and Feasibility of Agriculture and Rural Development Operations: How Economic Analyses Can Help, September 2005

   m. Assessing the Use of Project Distribution and Poverty Impact Analyses at the Asian Development Bank, October 2005

   n. Assessing Aid for a Sector Development Plan: Economic Analysis of a Sector Loan, November 2005

   o. Setting User Charges for Urban Water Supply: A Case Study of the Metropolitan Cebu Water District in the Philippines, June 2006

   p. Willingness-to-Pay and Design of Water Supply and Sanitation Projects: A Case Study, December 2006

   q. Tourism for Pro-Poor and Sustainable Growth: Economic Analysis of Tourism Projects, January 2007

   r. Good Practices for Estimating Reliable Willingness-to-Pay Values in the Water Supply and Sanitation Sector, December 2007

   s. Utility Tariff Setting for Economic Efficiency and Financial Sustainability: A Review, August 2008

Appendix 2:
Use of Constant Prices in the Economic Analysis of Projects

1.   Project economic analysis is conducted using constant prices (also termed real prices). Constant prices are current prices (also termed nominal prices) adjusted for the effect of general inflation, assuming that inflation will affect prices of all project inputs and outputs equally. Using constant prices ensures that the future costs and benefits of a project are comparable to those incurred at the time the decision to invest in the project is made.

Table A2: Commodity Price Projections in Current and Constant Prices

Commodity	Unit	2016	2017	2018	2019	2020	2021	2022
		Price Projection in Current US Dollars						
Coal, Australia	$/mt	51.0	51.9	52.9	53.8	54.8	55.8	56.8
Crude oil, average, spot	$/bbl	43.0	53.2	59.9	62.7	65.6	68.6	71.9
Sugar, World	$/kg	0.35	0.35	0.36	0.36	0.36	0.37	0.37
Rice, Thailand, 5%	$/mt	400	401	402	403	404	406	407
Wheat, US, HRW	$/mt	180	188	197	206	216	225	236
Palm oil	$/mt	650	665	681	697	713	729	747
Cotton A index	$/kg	1.55	1.61	1.68	1.74	1.81	1.88	1.96
Copper	$/mt	4,650	4,866	5,092	5,329	5,577	5,836	6,108
Urea, Eastern Europe bulk	$/mt	200	208	216	224	232	241	250
		Price Projection in 2016 Constant US Dollars						
Coal, Australia	$/mt	51.0	51.0	51.2	51.3	51.4	51.5	51.6
Crude oil, average, spot	$/bbl	43.0	52.3	58.0	59.7	61.5	63.3	65.3
Sugar, World	$/kg	0.35	0.34	0.35	0.34	0.34	0.34	0.34
Rice, Thailand, 5%	$/mt	400	394	389	384	379	375	370
Wheat, US, HRW	$/mt	180	185	191	196	203	208	214
Palm oil	$/mt	650	654	659	664	668	673	678
Cotton A index	$/kg	1.55	1.58	1.63	1.66	1.70	1.73	1.78
Copper	$/mt	4,650	4,785	4,928	5,076	5,229	5,385	5,548
Urea, Eastern Europe bulk	$/mt	200	205	209	213	218	222	227
Inflation index: MUV Index (2010=100)		100.0	101.7	103.3	105.0	106.7	108.4	110.1
Inflation rate: % change per annum		1.9	1.7	1.6	1.6	1.6	1.6	1.6

bbl = barrel, HRW = hard red winter, kg = kilogram, mt = metric ton, MUV = manufacturing unit value, US = United States.
Notes:
1.   Crude oil, average price of Brent Dubai and West Texas, Intermediate, equally weighed.
2.   MUV is the unit value index in US dollar terms of manufactures exported from 15 countries: Brazil, Canada, the People's Republic of China, Germany, France, India, Italy, Japan, Mexico, the Republic of Korea, South Africa, Spain, Thailand, the United kingdom, and the US.
Source: World Bank. 2016. Commodity Markets Outlook. 26 July.

2.   Table A2 compares constant and current price projections for a set of commodities. For traded items, the appropriate measure of inflation to adopt in adjusting current to constant prices is a measure of international inflation, such as the manufacturing unit value (MUV) index either of a single country, such as the United States, or an average of a number of countries. For nontraded items, an appropriate measure of inflation is the projected rate of increase in domestic prices, which can be a gross domestic product deflator, general consumer price index, or a more specific index such as a construction price index for construction costs.

3.   The use of constant prices removes the effects of general price increases. But it is possible that the relative prices of inputs and outputs could also change over time because of changes in productivity, technology, or demand. The price of a good may increase either slower or faster than the prices of other inputs and outputs, or vice versa. Expected changes in relative prices must also be reflected in project economic analysis.

4.   Suppose a 2.5% annual increase of nominal wages for unskilled labor over 5 years is expected, when the annual general price increase for the same period is projected at 12% per year—the change in the relative price of unskilled labor will be given by $(1 + 0.025) / (1 + 0.120) - 1 = -0.085$, or -8.5%. Therefore, the value of unskilled labor in constant prices should be reduced by 8.5% per year over the 5-year period. Alternatively, suppose there is a scarcity of skilled labor and wages are expected to increase by 15% per year for 5 years—if inflation is assumed at 12% per annum for the same period, then the price of scarce labor used in the analysis should be increased by 2.7% per year for 5 years, calculated from $(1 + 0.15) / (1 + 0.12) - 1 = 0.027$, or 2.7%.

Appendix 3:
Method for Constructing a Project Statement

1.   A project statement presents project economic costs and benefits in constant prices, and it provides a useful tool for project economic analysis. The statement can be drawn up for each subproject, each project alternative, and a project as a whole. The whole project statement will cover the implementation period of major investments and operating years. The number of operating years to be covered in the statement can be determined by

      a.   the technical life of the major investment assets, that is, the number of years of normal operation before the assets are fully worn out; or

      b.   the economic life of the same assets—the number of years after which annual operation and maintenance costs exceed annual gross benefits.

2.   Normally, the shorter of the two definitions of project life should be used. For some major economic infrastructure projects with particularly long lives, such as dams or railways, the project period may include 20–25 years of operation with the remaining life of assets represented by a residual value.

A.   Investment Costs

3.   Investment costs include initial investments to implement the project, replacement investments during the life of the project, and the residual value of investment assets at the end of the project. Initial investments are generally broken down into subcategories, such as land preparation, buildings and construction, equipment, vehicles, and other costs included in the initial investments such as environmental mitigation and monitoring. Physical contingencies included in the initial investments for economic analysis should be allocated to these different categories. The initial investments may be concentrated in a single project year, but are usually scheduled over more than 1 year according to the project phasing and implementation schedule.

4.   Associated with each subcategory of investment is a replacement period in years. On the assumption of normal maintenance activities, this replacement period indicates when the relevant assets will be worn out and will therefore need replacing. Typically, replacement investments, if required by design, are entered in the project statement in the last year of use of the current assets, when commitments to new resources have to be made. Different types of investment assets have different replacement periods.

5.   For whatever project period is decided upon, some assets will not be fully worn out at the end of the project period. The remaining value of the assets—their residual value—is entered as a negative investment cost at the end of the project. It can be calculated as the proportion of the replacement period still remaining for a particular subcategory, times the constant price value of the assets concerned.

6.   Table A3, Item A, illustrates the construction of an investment schedule for a processing project with an implementation period of 2 years and an operating period of 20 years based on the estimated project life. It includes the initial investments, the replacement investments at intervals, and the residual values of project assets at the end of the project life.

B.   Working Capital

7.   The processing project holds large initial stocks of raw materials at some times of the year, and no initial stocks at others. The supply is seasonal. An annual average amount for initial stocks and final stocks of output is included in Table A3, Item B, related to the capacity utilization of the assets. A residual value is included at the end of the project life. A more detailed treatment of working capital in project statements is illustrated in Appendix 6.

C.   Annual Benefits and Costs

8.   The supply of raw materials for the processing project builds up over 2 years from the end of implementation. Capacity utilization is 50% in the first operating year, and then 100% thereafter. Most annual costs (materials, utilities, and labor) are variable and increase with capacity utilization. Overhead costs are fixed. The annual costs include an estimate for the opportunity cost of land; half the land is taken over in the first implementation year, and the other half in the second year of implementation. The annual costs are totaled for each year of the project, as shown in Table A3, Item C.

9.   The processing project will be able to offer a better price for the local raw materials. It may take over some supplies at present going to local small-scale processors. However, most of the output will be from additional material supplies. The incremental output is built up with capacity utilization as in Table A3, Item D.

D.   Net Benefits

10.   The investment, working capital, and annual costs are subtracted from the incremental output for each year of the project life, as in Table A3, Item E. The net economic benefits are negative in the 2 implementation years, and in the later year in which the major equipment is replaced. They are low in the first operating year when the project is at less than full capacity utilization, and are high in the final year where they include the residual value of investment and working capital costs. Such a statement provides the basis on which a decision can be taken as to whether the future net benefits are a sufficient return for the earlier net costs.

Table A3: Project Statement
(in constant economic prices)

Item	Initial Amount (in $ million)	Replacement Period (in year)	0	1	2	3	4	5	6	7	8	9	10	11	12	13	14	15	16	17	18	19	20	21
Capacity Utilization					50%	100%	100%	100%	100%	100%	100%	100%	100%	100%	100%	100%	100%	100%	100%	100%	100%	100%	100%	100%
A. Investment Schedule																								
1. Land Preparation	80	–		80																				0
2. Construction	1,860	30	930	930																				(620)
3. Equipment	900	12		900												900								(300)
4. Vehicles	370	5		370					370					370					370					0
5. Others	60	–	30	30																				0
I. Total (1+2+3+4+5)	**3,270**		**960**	**2,310**	**0**	**0**	**0**	**0**	**370**	**0**	**0**	**0**	**0**	**370**	**0**	**900**	**0**	**0**	**370**	**0**	**0**	**0**	**0**	**(920)**
B. Working Capital																								
II. Total	**230**			**115**	**115**																			**(230)**
C. Annual Costs	Annual Amount																							
6. Materials	600				300	600	600	600	600	600	600	600	600	600	600	600	600	600	600	600	600	600	600	600

continued on next page

Table A3. continued

Years	Annual Amount	0	1	2	3	4	5	6	7	8	9	10	11	12	13	14	15	16	17	18	19	20	21
7. Utilities	170			85	170	170	170	170	170	170	170	170	170	170	170	170	170	170	170	170	170	170	170
8. Labor	145			73	145	145	145	145	145	145	145	145	145	145	145	145	145	145	145	145	145	145	145
9. Overheads	90			90	90	90	90	90	90	90	90	90	90	90	90	90	90	90	90	90	90	90	90
10. Land Opportunity	35	18	35	35	35	35	35	35	35	35	35	35	35	35	35	35	35	35	35	35	35	35	35
III. Total (6+7+8+9+10)	1,040	18	35	583	1,040	1,040	1,040	1,040	1,040	1,040	1,040	1,040	1,040	1,040	1,040	1,040	1,040	1,040	1,040	1,040	1,040	1,040	1,040
D. Benefits	Annual Amount																						
IV Incremental Output	1,695			848	1,695	1,695	1,695	1,695	1,695	1,695	1,695	1,695	1,695	1,695	1,695	1,695	1,695	1,695	1,695	1,695	1,695	1,695	1,695
E. Net Benefits (IV–I–II–III)		(978)	(2,460)	150	655	655	285	285	655	655	655	655	285	655	(245)	655	655	285	655	655	655	655	1,805
Discount Rate	9.00%																						
Net Present Value	1,158.8																						
Internal Rate of Return	13.46%																						

( ) = negative.
Source: ADB Economic Research and Regional Cooperation Department.

Appendix 4:
Consumer Surplus and Gross Project Economic Benefits

1.   Where demand is perfectly elastic, such as for most internationally traded goods, a project's output supply will not affect its market price, and no consumer surplus will be created as a result of the project. As illustrated In Figure A4.1, a project is represented by an outward shift in the supply curve from SS to S_1S_1. Assuming that all output is exported and is incremental, and all project output can be sold at the world price P_1, gross economic benefit will be the area ABQ_2Q_1 (where Q_1 is output supply without the project and Q_2 is output supply with the project). Ignoring transport and distribution costs and taxes and subsidies, the world price P_1 is the economic price, and the gross economic benefit (GEB) of the project output can be estimated as $GEB = P_1 \times (Q_2 - Q_1)$, where $Q_2 - Q_1$ is output supplied by the project.

Figure A4.1: Perfectly Elastic Demand Curve for Traded Goods

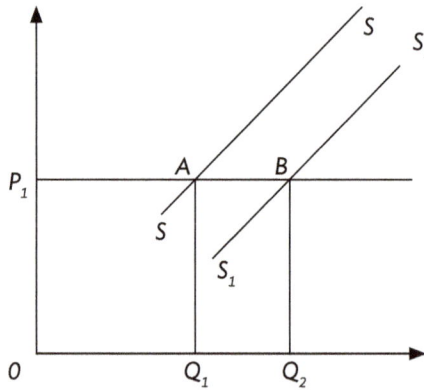

Source: ADB Economic Research and Regional Cooperation Department.

2.   However, where demand is less than perfectly elastic and the project faces a downward sloping demand curve, which is often the case for nontraded goods, output supply by a large project may reduce the market price. In that case, the price for project output actually paid by consumers is less than what they would be willing to pay, creating consumer surplus.

3.   In Figure A4.2, a good is sold domestically and faces less than perfectly elastic demand. The project shifts the supply curve from SS to S_1S_1, bringing

price down from P_1 (price without the project) to P_2 (price with the project) and increasing total demand from Q_1 (without the project) to Q_2 (with the project). The total output produced by the project is ($Q_2 - Q_3$), consisting of incremental output ($Q_2 - Q_1$) and nonincremental output ($Q_1 - Q_3$). The nonincremental output reflects the displaced production of the existing producers due to the lower market price as a result of the project.

Figure A4.2: Downward Sloping Demand Curve for Nontraded Goods

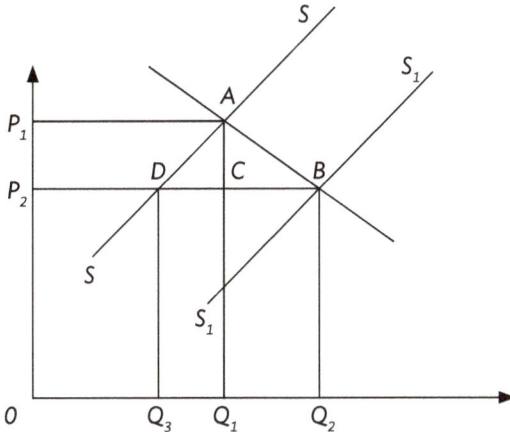

Source: ADB Economic Research and Regional Cooperation Department.

4.   In Figure A4.2, the gross economic benefit of the incremental output ($Q_2 - Q_1$) is the sum of the sales revenue denoted by the area of BQ_2Q_1C and consumer surplus denoted by the area ABC. This sum is consumers' willingness to pay for the incremental output. For the nonincremental output ($Q_1 - Q_3$), the gross economic benefit is the total cost savings from the displaced production of the existing producers, which is the entire area under the supply curve for the without project case (SS) and is denoted by ACQ_1Q_3D. The rectangular area P_1ACP_2 is also part of the consumer surplus created by the project. However, it consists of two parts: one part, area P_1ADP_2, reflects a loss in producer surplus (which is the difference between the market price actually paid by the consumers and production cost), and is a transfer from producers to consumers and should not be included in the project's gross economic benefit; the other part, area ACD, is included as part of the cost savings and, hence, is part of the gross economic benefit of the nonincremental output.

5.   Assuming that demand and supply curves are linear and prices charged for an output are market-clearing prices, that is, they are not depressed by regulation, consumer surplus associated with the incremental output, CS_{in}, can be approximated

by half of the product of the difference between without project and with project prices and the incremental output, that is

$$CS_{in} = \tfrac{1}{2}\,(P_1 - P_2) \times (Q_2 - Q_1) \tag{1}$$

The gross economic benefit of the incremental output, GEB_{in}, is therefore

$$GEB_{in} = \tfrac{1}{2}\,(P_1 - P_2) \times (Q_2 - Q_1) + P_2 \times (Q_2 - Q_1),\ \text{or}$$

$$GEB_{in} = \tfrac{1}{2}\,(P_1 + P_2) \times (Q_2 - Q_1). \tag{2}$$

6.   This shows that, with the above simplifying assumptions, the gross economic benefit of the incremental output can be estimated as the output quantity multiplied by the average of the prices with and without the project. Similarly, the gross economic benefit of the nonincremental output (or cost savings from the displaced production), GEB_{non}, can be approximated by

$$GEB_{non} = \tfrac{1}{2}\,(P1 - P2) \times (Q1 - Q3) + P2 \times (Q1 - Q3),\ \text{or}$$

$$GEB_{non} = \tfrac{1}{2}\,(P_1 + P_2) \times (Q_1 - Q_3). \tag{3}$$

7.   This shows that, with the above simplifying assumptions, the gross economic benefit of the nonincremental output can also be estimated as the output quantity multiplied by the average of the prices with and without the project. Total gross economic benefit of the project is therefore

$$GEB_{total} = \tfrac{1}{2}\,(P_1 + P_2) \times (Q_2 - Q_3). \tag{4}$$

8.   In the real world, however, because of various market distortions, such as taxes, subsidies, price controls, monopoly or monopsony power, and externalities, there is no reason why prices (P_1 and P_2 in Figure A4.2) should reflect consumers' marginal willingness to pay and marginal cost for producers. These distortions need to be adjusted for to arrive at true gross economic benefits of the project. In such cases, the calculation of economic benefits must be based on estimated economic prices, rather than using the prices actually obtained in the market (see Appendix 7 on deriving economic prices). For example, when output supply is rationed at a price below what buyers would be willing to pay, an increase in supply capacity at

the same price produces incremental consumer surplus, which is not captured by the average of with and without project output prices. In this case, it is necessary to estimate market-clearing prices with and without the project in order to apply equation (2). Similarly in the case of nonincremental output, the gross economic benefit (GEB_{non}) from equation (3) should be measured as cost savings per unit of output, and this must be approximated by the output quantity multiplied by the average of marginal economic costs with and without the project, rather than by the average of with and without market prices.

9.   The necessary adjustments for distortions will differ between incremental and nonincremental output. There is thus a need to divide total project output into incremental (expanding supply) and nonincremental (displacing existing supply) components. If price elasticity of demand and price elasticity of supply are known, the share of incremental output in total project output can be approximated by

$$Share_{in} = -\varepsilon_d / \left(-\varepsilon_d + \varepsilon_s\right) \qquad (5), and$$

similarly, the share of nonincremental output can be approximated by

$$Share_{non} = \varepsilon_s / \left(-\varepsilon_d + \varepsilon_s\right) \qquad (6)$$

where ε_d is price elasticity of demand (D) for the goods or services produced by the project, that is, percentage change in demand divided by percentage change in price, and is defined as

$$\varepsilon_d = (\Delta D/D) / (\Delta P/P) \qquad (7)$$

where Δ refers to a change in D or P. Similarly, ε_s is price elasticity of supply for the goods or services produced by the project, that is, percentage change in supply (S) divided by percentage change in price, and is defined as

$$\varepsilon_s = (\Delta S/S) / (\Delta P/P). \qquad (8)$$

10.   Insofar as supply elasticity tends to be lower than demand elasticity, a higher weight will be used for incremental output. Elasticity estimates will be subject to uncertainty and are likely to differ between the short run and the long run. For project analysis, approximate average estimates derived from secondary sources can be applied.

In many cases, projects supply services to new markets and empirical price-quantity data are not yet available. Market and user surveys have been used to provide willingness-to-pay data in such circumstances. Surveys can take the form of a contingent valuation when a respondent is asked what he or she would do in a hypothetical situation.

11.   Price elasticity of demand can sometimes be used to establish segments of a demand curve. In Figure A4.2, price elasticity of demand can be calculated as

$$\varepsilon_d = [(Q_2 - Q_1)/Q_1]/[(P_1 - P_2)/P_1] \tag{9}$$

If ε_d can be established from secondary sources, and Q_1, Q_2, and P_1 (or P_2) are known, P_2 (or P_1) can be calculated approximately from the above equation.[1]

---

[1]   For large changes in price, the relevant price elasticity is an arc elasticity where changes in both price and quantity are relative to the average of the with and without project case, that is

$\varepsilon_d = [(Q_2 - Q_1)/(Q_1 + Q_2)/2]/[(P_1 - P_2)/(P_1 + P_2)/2]$.

Appendix 5:
Methods for Valuing Nonmarket Impacts

1.   Four groups of methods are discussed: stated preference, revealed preference, physical linkage (or dose–response functions), and benefit transfer.

A.   Stated Preference Methods

2.   Stated preference methods elicit consumers' willingness to pay for changes in the quantity or quality of nonmarket goods and services provided by a project. There are two main stated preference methods: contingent valuation and choice modeling.

Contingent Valuation

3.   Contingent valuation (CV) involves a survey directly asking people how much they would be willing to pay for specific goods or services in a specific but hypothetical situation. The word "contingent" is used because of the hypothetical nature of the scenarios presented to the respondents. In nearly all situations where a survey can be conducted, CV can be performed. CV has been used in many applications including issues related to water supply, sanitation, energy, health, and the environment.[1]

4.   A CV study usually involves the following steps:

Step 1: The benefits to be valued are defined and beneficiary populations for each type of benefit are identified. The expected change in nonmarket services for each beneficiary population is quantified.

Step 2: Sampling for the survey is designed to allow statistical testing. Sampling should be representative, and, at a minimum, should be sufficient to allow prediction of values for the population via estimated coefficients.

Step 3: The survey is designed. A key issue is how the question related to willingness to pay is presented to respondents. There are three ways to do so: (1) *open-ended* where the respondent is asked to "state" their highest willingness to pay; (2) *close-ended* where the respondent is presented with a randomly varied specific number and is asked whether or not he/she would be willing to pay this amount; and (3) *payment card* where the respondent is presented with a menu of (often randomly

---

[1]   Examples of applying the CV method to water and sanitation projects are provided in Chapters 4 and 5 of ADB. 2013. *Cost–Benefit Analysis for Development: A Practical Guide.* Manila. Environmental Valuation & Cost–Benefit News at http://www.envirovaluation.org/ provides references to several empirical studies using CV.

varied) potential payments and is asked to indicate the highest value he/she would be willing to pay.

5.　　One limitation of the CV method is that it could be susceptible to hypothetical bias where respondents state higher willingness to pay than is actually demonstrated in behavior. This may be because of strategic behavior, where respondents know that high values increase the likelihood of project provision, but have no impact on actual charges, or where they consider this to be the socially acceptable position. There are two ways to counter this: (1) make the survey appear consequential, so that responses may be binding; and (2) ask about the certainty of responses during the survey (via "certainty scales"), and use this information in the analysis of responses.

6.　　Data on other variables that affect willingness to pay should also be included in the survey. Income will normally be an important determinant and may need to be approximated by information on consumption. Information will typically be required on factors like education level, exposure to the affected service, ownership of assets, and investment in mitigation/substitution measures.

Step 4: The survey is implemented, almost always in person. To assure quality, this requires detailed training of enumerators, followed by their close oversight by the lead expert.

Step 5: Data are analyzed using an appropriate regression framework to identify willingness to pay and the effects of the controlling variables.

Choice Modeling

7.　　Choice modeling (CM) uses comparisons among alternative options to examine preferences in the context of trade-offs. CM has many variants, including choice experiments, choice ranking, discrete choice modeling, and conjoint analysis. CM has been used for a wide range of nonmarket benefits and can be potentially employed in any context where CV is used. It is particularly useful when the intention is to understand the value of multiple attributes of a nonmarket service.[2]

8.　　The strength of CM is that, while hypothetical, it can be anchored to real world trade-offs and choices. For example, several options of an environmental program, with different attributes, can be compared with the status quo. Respondents can then be surveyed to establish the probability that they will select each option above the others. These probabilities can then be explained in a statistical model by the

---

[2]　For example, choice modeling has been used to assess preferences for natural assets: Hanley, N., S. Mourato, and R. E. Wright. 2001. *Choice Modelling Approaches: A Superior Alternative for Environmental Valuation? Journal of Economic Surveys.* 15. pp. 435–462.

measurable attributes of each option (such as impact on air pollution, litter, or sewage plus their cost). The coefficients of the model can be used to infer a price for each of the attribute, which in turn can be used to derive an estimate of willingness to pay for each option. The approach has the advantage over CV of allowing a comparison between a set of alternatives, rather than simply valuing one option and can isolate the value of the different attributes of options. However, like CV studies, CM studies also need to be designed carefully and may not be free from bias.

B.   Revealed Preference Methods

9.   Revealed preference methods infer values from actual individual behavior, so that hypothetical bias is eliminated. Their weakness is that actual behavioral patterns may be affected by unobserved variables. There are several variants of revealed preference methods.

Hedonic Pricing

10.   Hedonic pricing is based on the assumption that when individuals buy a good or a service, the price they are willing to pay depends on the characteristics of the good or service. The method isolates the contribution of each of these individual characteristics to the market price of the good or service. For example, the market price of a real estate property may depend in part on the level of environmental quality, and of a hotel room may depend upon proximity to a natural attraction.

11.   The hedonic pricing method is used to isolate the value of nonmarket amenities as they contribute to price levels. Having isolated such a value, it is then possible to estimate the value of a specific change in those amenities. Many applications of the hedonic pricing method use variations in residential housing prices to estimate the value of environmental amenities.[3] While the hedonic pricing method is intuitively easy to understand, its application requires considerable statistical expertise to ensure that all other influences on price, other than the effect of interest, have been controlled for.

Averting Expenditures

12.   The averting expenditure (sometimes termed the defensive expenditure) method is based on the presumption that people will change their behavior and invest to avoid an undesirable environmental impact. Examples could be the installation of double-glazed windows to reduce exposure to road traffic noise or the purchase of water filters or purification systems to avoid using polluted water. In the first case, the

---

[3]   See, for example, Tyrväinen, L. 1997. *The amenity value of the urban forest: an application of the hedonic pricing method. Landscape and Urban Planning.* 37 (3). pp. 211–222.

cost needed for installing the double-glazed windows can be used as a proxy for the value of reduced exposure to noise; in the second case, the cost needed for installing water filters or purification systems could be considered as a proxy for the value of using safe water.[4]

13.   The averting expenditure method, although simple to implement, is subject to a number of complications. First, such expenditure may represent only a partial estimate of the value of a nonmarket impact, if the impact cannot be averted entirely. Second, many averting behaviors are related to joint products (e.g., heating and insulation from noise in the case of double-glazed windows). Third, people may undertake more than one form of averting behavior in response to nonmarket impacts, and in such case, all forms of averting expenditures should be considered.

C.   Physical Linkage Methods

14.   The physical linkage methods (sometimes called dose–response functions) focus on measuring physical relationships between nonmarket impacts and effects felt in other markets, with consequences for marketed activity, usually in terms of changes in outputs of production or costs. For instance, a decrease in water quality due to pollution can have an adverse impact on fish stock in terms of quantity and/or quality. Benefits of improved water quality can be approximated by avoided loss of fish production.[5] Another example is air pollution causing human illness that leads to more treatment costs and production losses. The avoided treatment costs and production losses provide approximations to economic benefits of air pollution control.[6]

D.   Benefit Transfer Method

15.   The benefit transfer method can be used to estimate economic values of nonmarket goods or services by transferring information from studies already completed in other project sites or locations and using these values for the problem under examination.

---

[4]   See, for example, Um, M., S. Kwak, and T. Y. Kim. 2002. *Estimating Willingness to Pay for Improved Drinking Water Quality Using Averting Behavior Method with Perception Measure.* Environmental and Resource Economics. 21. p. 285.

[5]   See, for example, Barbier, E. 2007. *Valuing Ecosystem Services as Productive Inputs.* Economic Policy. 22 (49). pp. 177–229.

[6]   See ADB. 2009. *The Economics of Climate Change in Southeast Asia: A Regional Review.* Manila (Chapter 4: Modeling Climate Change and Its Impact, pages 62–81); and Stern Review: The Economics of Climate Change. http://mudancasclimaticas.cptec.inpe. br/~rmclima/pdfs/destaques/sternreview_report_complete.pdf.

16.   The benefit transfer method can either take the form of a transfer of a unit value (for example, value per hectare of forest or value per cubic meter of avoided erosion) or the transfer of functional relationship between projects or locations. The unit value transfer involves using benefit estimates (such as willingness to pay) from existing studies or from similar projects for use by the project under examination. Where necessary, the transferred values should be adjusted to allow for differences between the project site and comparison study. These adjustments are best done when the transfer involved is not of a unit value but of a functional relationship between a price and characteristics of the study area, like income or pollution levels. The benefit function transfer involves transferring benefit functions estimated elsewhere and is usually more accurate because it allows for differences in socioeconomic characteristics that influence benefit values.

17.   Benefit transfer is usually carried out in three steps. First, existing literature on the subject under investigation is compiled, such as for example, recreational activity, human health, or air and water pollution. Second, selected studies are assessed for their comparability with the problem under consideration (for example, similarity of the environmental services to be valued and any differences in income, education, age, and other characteristics of those affected by these services). Third, values are adjusted to ensure comparability.

18.   Benefit transfer can avoid data collection and processing costs and can be used to obtain approximations of the possible extent of nonmarket costs or benefits. It is often an adequate approach where the nonmarket impact on either the benefit or cost side is relatively small. Where the nonmarket impact is significant, for example, in environmental improvement projects, use of a benefit transfer approach could potentially be misleading and direct valuation estimates will be required.[7]

---

[7]   Bergstrom, J. C. and L. O. Taylor. 2006. *Using meta-analysis for benefits transfer: Theory and practice. Ecological Economics.* 60 (2). pp. 351–360.

Appendix 6:
Treatment of Working Capital

1.   Most projects require physical stocks of goods both as outputs (held before their final sale and distribution) and inputs (including materials and spare parts and those tied up in partially completed production) for continued operations. These are part of working capital and should be allowed for in the project economic analysis. They are shown separately from the annual project costs for operation and maintenance. The financial aspects of working capital covering funds held for financing purposes and the net creditor/debtor position of a project in relation to suppliers/purchasers are not included in the economic costs of working capital.

2.   The value of working capital is calculated at constant economic prices. If the level of stocks varies over the year, as for many agriculture-based activities, annual average stock levels are used in the calculations. Since costs of materials, spares, work in progress, and finished outputs as working capital will all be recovered after final sale of outputs, only the initial stocks and annual changes in working capital are entered in project economic analysis. In addition, the total stocks held as working capital are released at the end of the project, so they should be shown as a residual value and deducted from production costs.

3.   Table A6 provides an example of how working capital is treated for a project with a 1-year construction period and a 10-year operation period, on the basis of the assumptions below:
   a.   Capacity utilization for the project builds up over 3 years at utilization rates of 50%, 80%, and 100%, and then is sustained at maximum capacity.
   b.   The annual fixed operating costs, including administrative labor and non-tradable items for office supplies, are 150.
   c.   The annual variable operating costs at the full capacity utilization are 372, consisting of 252 for materials, 60 for utilities, and 60 for labor.

4.   The calculations are as follows:
   a.   Fixed operating costs will be 150 each from year 1 to 10.
   b.   Materials will be 252 × 50% = 126 for year 1, 252 × 80% = 202 for year 2 and 252 × 100% =252 for years 3–10
   c.   Utilities will be 60 × 50% = 30 for year 1, 60 × 80% = 48 for year 2, and 60 × 100% = 60 for years 3-10
   d.   Labor will be 60 × 50% = 30 for year 1, 60 × 80% = 48 for year 2, and 60 × 100% = 60 for years 3–10

5.   The calculations to arrive at the working capital are as follows:
     a.   Initial stocks at the full capacity utilization are 2 months' worth of
          materials and spares at 252 × 2/12 = 42. The figure is 21 at 50% capacity
          utilization and 33.6 at 80% utilization. The change in the initial stocks is
          therefore 21 in year 0, 12.6 in year 1, 8.4 in year 2, zero for years 3–9, and
          −42 (residual value) in year 10.
     b.   Final stocks at the full capacity are 1 month's worth of sales at cost at
          522/12 = 43.5. The figure is 21.75 at 50% utilization in year 1 and 34.8
          at 80% utilization in year 2. The change in the final stocks is therefore
          21.75 in year 1, 13.05 in year 2, 8.70 in year 3, and 0 in years 4–9, and
          −43.50 in year 10.
     c.   Cost related to work in progress at the full capacity utilization is
          calculated on the basis of 20 days out of 250 working days per year
          and covers the material costs and half of utility and labor costs, that
          is, [252 + 0.5 × (522–252–150)] × (20/250) = 24.96 and the figure is
          12.48 at 50% utilization, 19.97 at 80% utilization, and 24.96% at 100%
          utilization. The change in work in progress is therefore 12.48 in year 1,
          7.49 in year 2, 4.99 in year 3, 0 in years 4–9, and −24.96 in year 10.
     d.   The total change in working capital is 21 in year 0, 46.83 year 1, 28.94 in
          year 2, 13.69 in year 3, 0 in years 4–9, and −110.43 in year 10.

Table A6: Calculation of Changes in Working Capital
(at economic costs)

Years		0	1	2	3	4	5	6	7	8	9	10
Capacity Utilization	A	0%	50%	80%	100%	100%	100%	100%	100%	100%	100%	100%
Operating Costs												
Fixed	B		150.00	150.00	150.00	150.00	150.00	150.00	150.00	150.00	150.00	150.00
Variable – Materials	C		126.00 (252×50%)	201.60 (252×80%)	252.00 (252×100%)	252.00	252.00	252.00	252.00	252.00	252.00	252.00
– Utilities	D		30.00 (60×50%)	48.00 (60×80%)	60.00 (60×100%)	60.00	60.00	60.00	60.00	60.00	60.00	60.00
– Labor	E		30.00 (60×50%)	48.00 (60×80%)	60.00 (60×100%)	60.00	60.00	60.00	60.00	60.00	60.00	60.00
Total	**F=B+C+D+E**		**336.00**	**447.60**	**522.00**	**522.00**	**522.00**	**522.00**	**522.00**	**522.00**	**522.00**	**522.00**
Working Capital												
Initial Stocks	G	21.00 (252×2/12×50%)	33.60 (252×2/12×80%)	42.00 (252×2/12×100%)	42.00	42.00	42.00	42.00	42.00	42.00	42.00	–
Change in Initial Stocks	H	21.00	12.60 (G1–G0)	8.40 (G2–G1)	0 (G3–G2)	0	0	0	0	0	0	(42.00) (G10–G9)
Final Stocks	I		21.75 (522/12×50%)	34.80 (522/12×80%)	43.50 (522/12×100%)	43.50	43.50	43.50	43.50	43.50	43.50	–
Change in Final Stock	J		21.75 (I1–I0)	13.05 (I2–I1)	8.70 (I3–I2)	0 (I4–I3)	0	0	0	0	0	(43.50) (I10–I9)

continued on next page

Table A6. continued

Years		0	1	2	3	4	5	6	7	8	9	10
Work in Progress	K		12.48 [252 + 0.5 × (522–252–150)] × (20/250) × 50%	19.97 [252 + 0.5 × (522–252–150)] × (20/250) × 80%	24.96 [252 + 0.5 × (522–252–150)] × (20/250) × 100%	24.96	24.96	24.96	24.96	24.96	24.96	–
Change in Work in Progress	L		12.48 (K1–K0)	7.49 (K2–K1)	4.99 (K3–K2)	0 (K4–K3)	0	0	0	0	0	(24.96) (K10–K9)
Total Change in Working Capital	K=H+J+L	21.00	46.83	28.94	13.69	0	0	0	0	0	0	(110.46)

– = not applicable, ( ) = negative.
Source: ADB Economic Research and Regional Cooperation Department.

Appendix 7:
Examples of Deriving Economic Prices

A.   Traded Goods and Services

1.   Three cases are illustrated below: an export output, an import substitute output, and an imported input. The official exchange rate (OER) is L10/$ and shadow exchange rate (SER) is estimated to be L11/$, so shadow exchange rate factor (SERF) is 1.1. The illustrations are given using a domestic price numeraire with a SERF of 1.1. The illustrations use local currency (denoted as L).

B.   Case 1: Economic Price of an Export Output

2.   Palm oil is exported at a free on board (FOB) price of $100 per ton. There are distribution and transport costs in local currency (L) of L30 and L60, respectively, in moving the palm oil from the project to the border, and an export tax of 5% of the FOB value.

3.   The financial price of palm oil to the project is the FOB price at OER less export tax and the local costs (distribution and transport costs)[1] of moving it to the port. When using the domestic price numeraire, the economic price at the project site is the FOB price revalued by SER less the export tax (as this is a transfer payment, the conversion factor is zero) and the economic costs of distribution and transport (the latter being the financial costs minus the tax component in transport).[2] The economic price is L1,015 (see Table A7.1).

---

[1]   The assumed tax on transport cost is 9%.
[2]   In principle, had more information been available and their costs sufficiently high to warrant closer attention, distribution and transport could have been decomposed further into traded, nontraded, labor, and transfer components with each revalued by the appropriate conversion factor (CF).

Table A7.1: Illustration of Export Product: Palm Oil

Cost Item	Financial Price (L/ton)	Conversion Factor	Economic Price (L/ton)
Palm oil at port	1,000	1.1	1,100
Less:			
Export tax	50	0	0
Distribution cost	30	1.0	30
Transport cost of which:	60		55
Tax	5	0	0
Others	55	1.0	55
Total cost: Palm oil at the project	**860**		**1,015**

L= local currency.
Notes:
1. Economic price of palm oil: Palm oil at L100/ton × 10 tons × 1.1 = L1,100.
2. Export tax at 5% of FOB: L1,000 × 5% = L50; economic price is 0.
3. Economic price of distribution cost: L30 × 1 = L30.
4. Economic price of transport cost:
    Tax: L5/L55 = 0.09 or 9%; L55 × 9% = L5.
    Others: L60–L5 = L55; L55 × 1 = L55.
5. Economic price of palm oil at the project: L1,100 – L30 – L55 = L1,015.
Source: ADB Economic Research and Regional Cooperation Department.

C.   Case 2: Economic Price of an Import Substitute Output

4.   Irrigation pumps are assembled domestically and replace imports. The cost, insurance, and freight (CIF) value per pump is $200 and is subject to a 20% import tariff. Domestic production saves the cost of moving imported pumps from the port to the market, which is L100 per pump in distribution cost and L80 per pump in transport cost (inclusive of 9.5% tax). However, the pumps from the project must now be moved to the local market at a cost of L20 in distribution and L50 (inclusive of an 8% tax) in transport. The pumps from the project are priced to match the cost of imports in the local market. This means the price is determined by the CIF price of L2,000 ($10 at OER) plus a 20% import duty plus transport and distribution of L180 to give a financial price set by the project of L2,580. However, net revenue received by the project will be lower at L2,510 as the costs of moving the output from the project to the local market of L70 must be deducted. To calculate the economic price, the CIF price is first adjusted by the SERF, then the distribution and transportation cost of moving the pump from the port to the local market are added (taxes associated with transport are excluded as they are transfer payments and, because computation is in the domestic price numeraire, the appropriate conversion factor is 1). Finally, cost of moving the output from the project site to the local market is subtracted (once again, taxes associated with transport are excluded as they are transfer payments and, because computation is in the domestic price numeraire, the appropriate conversion factor is 1). The economic price of the pump is L2,307 (see Table A7.2).

Table A7.2: Illustration of Import Substitute Product: Pump

	Financial Price	Conversion Factor	Economic Price
Pump at port	L2,000	1.1	L2,200
Plus			
Import tariff	L400	0.0	0
Distribution cost	L100	1.0	L100
Transport cost of which:	L80		L73
Tax	L7	0.0	0
Others	L73	1.0	L73
Less cost from project to market	L70		L66
Distribution cost	L20	1.0	L20
Transport cost of which:	L50		
Tax	L4	0.0	0
Others	L46	1.0	L46
Price at port	**L2,510**		**L2,307**

L= local currency.
Notes:
A. Cost of moving pumps from port to market:
1. Economic price of pump: L2,000 × 10 × 1.1 = L2,200.
2. Import tax at 20% of CIF: L200 × 20% = L40; economic price = 0.
3. Economic price of distribution cost: L100 × 1 = L100.
4. Economic price of transport cost:
   Tax: L7/L73 = 0 .095 or 9.5%; L73 × 9.5% = L7.
   Others: L60 – L5 = L55; L55 × 1 = L55.
B. Cost of moving pumps from project to market
5. Economic price of distribution cost: L20 × 1 = L20.
6. Economic price of transport cost:
   Tax: L4/L46 = 0.087 or approximately 9%; L46 × 8.7% = L4.
   Others: L50–L4 = L46; L46 × 1 = L46.
C. Economic price of pump at port: L2,200 + (L100+L73) – (L20+L46) = L2,307
Source: ADB Economic Research and Regional Cooperation Department.

D.   Case 3: Economic Cost of an Imported Input

5.   A truck is imported for use on a project at a CIF price of $40,000. It is subject to both an import duty of 20% and an excise duty of 10%. The cost of distribution and transport in moving it from the port to the project is L1,000 and L2,000 (inclusive of 8.3% tax), respectively. The financial cost to the project is the CIF price L400,000 ($40,000 at OER of L10/$) plus the taxes and the distribution and transport cost, amounting to L523,000.

6.   To compute the economic price, the financial price is adjusted by the SERF and transport and distribution costs are added. The latter are not adjusted with conversion factors as they are in domestic prices. Import tariff, excise duty, and taxes associated with transport are excluded as they are transfer payments. The economic cost of L442,833 is well below the financial cost because of the omission

of taxes, principally on the imported truck itself—as transfers, these are not economic costs (see Table A7.3).

Table A7.3: Illustration of Import Product: Truck

	Financial Price	Conversion Factor	Economic Price
Truck at port	L400,000	1.1	L440,000
Plus			
Import tariff	L80,000	0	0
Excise duty	L40,000	0	0
Distribution cost	L1,000	1.0	L1,000
Transport cost of which	L2,000		L1,833
Tax	L167	0	0
Others	L1,833	1.0	L1,833
Truck at project	L523,000		L442,833

L= local currency.
Notes:
1. Economic price of truck at port: L40,000 × L10 (OER) × 1.1 = L440,000.
2. Import tariff at 20%: L400,000 × 20% = L80,000.
3. Excise duty at 10%: L400,000 × 10% = L40,000.
4. Economic price of distribution cost: L1,000 × 1 = L1,000.
5. Economic prince of transport cost:
    Tax: L167/L1,833 = 0.91 or 9%; L1,833 × 9.1% = L167.
    Others: L2,000 – L167=L1,833; L1,833 × 1 = L1,833.
6. Economic price of the truck at the project: L440,000 + L1,000 + L1,833 = L442,833.
Source: ADB Economic Research and Regional Cooperation Department.

E.   Nontraded Goods and Services

7.   Three examples are given here to illustrate the derivation of economic prices or costs for nontraded items: a nontraded output with both incremental and nonincremental effects, a nontraded input with incremental effects, and a nontraded input whose use by a project diverts the good from other users. As before, a SERF of 1.1 is assumed, with economic prices and costs given in units of local currency (L).

F.   Case 1: Nontraded Output - Bus Services

8.   A project expands bus services in an urban area to reduce the journey cost. Without the project, users will rely on shared minibuses. The market for bus services has been assessed by a passenger survey. Approximate demand and supply elasticities are available from a secondary source: –1.4 for the price elasticity of demand and 0.5 for the price elasticity of supply. These give a weight of 0.74 for incremental output[3] and 0.26 for nonincremental output.[4]

---

[3]   Calculated as 0.74 = [–(–1.4)/(–(–1.4)+0.5)] using equation 5 of Appendix 4.
[4]   Calculated as 0.26 = [(0.5)/(–(–1.4)+0.5)] using equation 6 of Appendix 4.

9.   For nonincremental output, financial cost per kilometer (km) for riding a representative minibus is L9 and is determined principally by fuel used (inclusive of the 20% tax), labor time of the driver, and wear and tear of the vehicle. These costs must be revalued to reflect the economic prices of the inputs. When using the domestic price numeraire, a SERF of 1.1 is applied to all traded costs, and the cost of driver's time is valued at a shadow wage rate factor (SWRF) of 0.5 to reflect significant unemployment in the area, to give the economic cost for taking a minibus as L7.5/km (see Table A7.4).

Table A7.4: Illustration of Economic Cost per Kilometer of Minibus Service: Nonincremental Output

	Financial Cost/km	Conversion Factor	Economic Cost/km
Fuel, of which	L6		
Traded cost	L5	1.1	L5.5
Tax	L1	0	0
Labor cost	L2	0.5	L1
Other nontraded costs	L1	1.0	L1
Total cost	**L9**		**L7.5**

km= kilometer, L= local currency.
Source: ADB Economic Research and Regional Cooperation Department.

10.   The incremental journeys induced by the project are valued at what passengers are willing to pay. The without project price is taken as the equivalent cost per km by minibus of L9 and the with project cost is the proposed average fare per km of L4. The average of these two prices, L6.5, is used to approximate average willingness to pay.

11.   The average economic price per km of passenger journey for the total project output can be calculated as a weighted average of the average economic cost for the nonincremental output and average economic price of the incremental output with the weights determined by the respective price elasticities. The weighted average economic price per km of passenger journey for the total project output is L6.76 in the domestic price numeraire (see Table A7.5). Using the domestic price numeraire, the gross economic benefit of the project can be estimated as the product of L6.76 and total kilometers of passenger journeys produced by the project.

Table A7.5: Weighted Average Economic Price per Kilometer of Passenger Journey for Bus Services

	Basis of Valuation	Weight	Economic Price/Cost	Weighted Average Economic Price
Nonincremental output	Cost savings on minibus	0.26	L7.5	L1.95
Incremental output	Willingness to pay for bus travel	0.74	L6.5	L4.81
Economic price				L6.76
Financial price				L4.00

L= local currency.
Notes:
1. Weight of nonincremental output: 0.5 / [0.5 – (–1.4)] = 0.26.
2. Weight of incremental output: – (–1.4) / [0.5 – (–1.4)] = 0.74.
3. Weighted average economic price for nonincremental output:
   Economic costs/km × weight for nonincremental output: L7.5 × 0.26 = L1.95.
4. Weighted average economic price for incremental output:
   WTP × weight for the incremental output: L6.5 × 0.74 = L4.81 where WTP is the average of the cost per km by minibus (L9) and the proposed average fare per km of L4.
5. Economic Price: L1.95 + L4.81 = L6.76.
Source: ADB Economic Research and Regional Cooperation Department.

G. Case 2: Nontraded Input in Incremental Supply – Power Project

12. Where a nontraded input has its production expanded to meet project demand, economic price is set by the per unit marginal cost of this extra production. Where power supplies are expanded to meet project demand, economic valuation requires estimating cost per kilowatt-hour (kWh) and decomposing this into its different elements, which are then revalued at economic prices. Here, the cost of supply is decomposed into fuel, labor, capital charges, other miscellaneous nontraded inputs, and taxes. The SERF of 1.1 is used. All labor is treated as skilled labor in scarce supply, so the conversion factor (CF) is 1.0. Power is sold to the project at a tariff of L160/kWh, although costs at financial prices come to L170, so there is a subsidy of L10/kWh. The nontraded inputs that cannot be decomposed further are valued at a CF of 1.0. The financial subsidy is treated as a transfer and like taxes is removed from the calculation. The result is a revalued economic cost of power of L173/kWh (see Table A7.6).

Table A7.6: Illustration of Economic Price for a Power Project

Project Inputs	Financial Cost Breakdown (L/kWh)	Conversion Factor	Economic Price (L/kWh)
Fuel – traded, of which	L80		
Traded CIF	L70	1.1	L77
Tax	L10	0.0	0
Labor	L10	1.0	L10
Capital charge			
Traded CIF	L60	1.1	L66
Nontraded	L10	1.0	L10
Miscellaneous inputs – nontraded	L10	1.0	L10
Subsidy	(L10)	0.0	0
Price to project	L160		L173

( ) = negative; CIF = cost, insurance, and freight; kWh = kilowatt-hour; L= local currency.
Notes:
1. Economic price of traded fuel, CIF × SERF: L70 × 1.1 = L77.
2. Taxes on fuel = 17.2%; L10/L70 = 0.172.
3. Economic price of labor: L10 × 1 = L10.
4. Economic price of capital charge, traded CIF cost × SERF: L 60 × 1.1 = L66.
5. Economic price of capital charge, nontraded cost: L10 × 1 = L10.
6. Total cost of power in economic prices: L77 + L10 + L66 + L10 + L10 = L173.
Source: ADB Economic Research and Regional Cooperation Department.

H. Case 3: Nontraded Input in Nonincremental Supply – Water Project

13. Water is diverted from agricultural use to a new project and its value to farmers can be approximated by the costs they are willing to incur to access alternative sources of water. The total cost per cubic meters (m^3) of water for digging a well or relocating an irrigation canal discounted over the life of the well or canal divided by the discounted stream of water produced over the working life (average incremental cost) gives an estimate of willingness to pay. The costs of the investment should be at financial prices, as this reflects what a farmer would be willing to spend to retain access to the water. Here, the average incremental cost of providing water by alternative means to farmers is L18/m^3, although the project using the diverted water will pay a tariff of L10/m^3. In this case, willingness to pay in a domestic price numeraire is the cost of the alternative supply source of L18 (Table A7.7).

Table A7.7: Illustration of Economic Price for a Nonincremental Water Supply Project

Cost of Alternative Source	Financial Prices (L/m³)	Economic Price
Present value capital cost	L10	
Present value operating cost	L8	
Total cost (cost of alternative supply)	L18	L18
Price to project – Assumed actual tariff	L10	

m³ = cubic meter, L = local currency.
Source: ADB Economic Research and Regional Cooperation Department.

Appendix 8:
Illustrations of Estimating
the Shadow Wage Rate

A. Example 1

1.   A project recruits unskilled workers from the surrounding areas, where they would previously have been working on a daily basis as casual unskilled workers. The project now offers full-time employment for 3 years. It is assumed that daily wages for casual workers reflect productivity per day in their without project activity. Days per month of casual work times the average casual wage gives monthly casual earnings. There is open unemployment in some months of the year. Allowing for this, the total annual casual earnings are L1,436 (L is the unit of local currency). If the project offers a full time wage of L150 per month based on the minimum wage regulations, this gives an annual wage of L1,800. The ratio of the shadow wage to the project wage, or the shadow wage rate factor, is then L1,436/L1,800 = 0.80 (see Table A8).

Table A8: Illustration of Shadow Wage
(in unit of local currency)

Month	Casual Wage per Day	Person-days Working per Month	Monthly Casual Earnings
January	12	20	240
February	12	18	216
March	10	15	150
April	10	14	140
May	10	14	140
June	5	0	0.0
July	5	0	0.0
August	5	0	0.0
September	8	10	80
October	8	10	80
November	10	15	150
December	12	20	240
Total		**136**	**1,436**

Source: ADB Economic Research and Regional Cooperation Department.

B.   Example 2

2.   A project offers a wage of L120/month, which includes a 20% premium on the wage offered elsewhere for the same skills; 70% of the workers it employs are drawn from other employers who pay a wage of L100/month. The remaining 30% of employees would otherwise be out of work living either on informal sector activities or on government unemployment benefits. The minimum they would accept to work for is determined by their other sources of income and, on average, this is assumed to be L30/month. In this case, the shadow wage will be $0.7 \times 100 + 0.3 \times 30 = 79$. As the wage paid by the project is L120, this gives a shadow wage rate factor of L79/L120 = 0.66.

Appendix 9:
Economic Price of Land
and Treatment of Resettlement

A.   Economic Price of Land

1.   Nearly all projects involve an additional use of land. Whether land is purchased or allocated to a project, it has an economic cost. The economic cost of land should be included in the project resource flow for calculating the economic internal rate of return. The first step in calculating the economic cost of land is to analyze the changes in land use that the project or project alternative will bring about. Some rehabilitation projects may require no additional land and therefore no change in land use. Expansion or new projects will require a land allocation and therefore a change in land use. Where existing activities are displaced and not terminated, there will also be an indirect change in land use at the site to which they are relocated. A survey is therefore required for

   a.   demarcation of the project's full land requirement,
   b.   demarcation of land required for relocation,
   c.   identifying those areas where land use will not change, and
   d.   identifying those areas where land use will change.

2.   The economic price of land is based on those areas where there will be a change in land use. The use of this land without the project provides the basis for its economic price. The without project situation should be based on the next best use of this land area. The basic measure to use as the cost of the land where use is changing is the value of output, net of all inputs, including labor and equipment that would be produced on the land without the project. This opportunity cost of the land should be measured at economic prices. Because of current trends or expected changes in the future, the opportunity cost per unit of land may change in the without project situation. Land productivity may increase where new agricultural methods can be anticipated or where infrastructure investments are planned. Land productivity may decline where, for example, soil erosion or exhaustion is occurring or where rainfall is becoming scarcer. The net output of the land in the without project situation should be estimated for each year of the project.

3.   The opportunity cost of land will differ from place to place. In broad terms, a distinction can be made between changing land use in rural areas, where agricultural production will be lost; in city areas, where a range of services and activities may be displaced; and in special development zones, where the production structure is changing rapidly.

4.   In rural areas, changes in land use will result in lost agricultural production. The existing land use should be assessed and a land suitability analysis carried out for the best without project alternative. Commonly, a specific product or small number of products will be selected to represent the lost net output from the land. Estimates can be made on a per hectare basis and then projected onto the total land area. Where it is observed that agricultural techniques or cropping patterns are changing, an annual adjustment to the lost output per hectare can be made to reflect changing productivities.

5.   In city areas, for example, because of the construction of a new ring road, the effects are more complex. There may be several types of service or activity being displaced by the project. It is more likely that the displaced activities will be relocated where there are already existing activities, and so the estimation of opportunity cost of land in the project area and in the area of relocation can be equally complex. The economic price of the land is the summation of the several changes in land use measured according to the type of activity being displaced. Table A9 illustrates the possibilities for a road project in an urban area. It specifies the present or without project use of land, the areas of land where land use will change, the area of relocation for displaced activities, and the method of estimating the opportunity cost of the land occupied by different activities without the project.

Table A9: Possible Urban Land-Use Changes of a Road Project

Without Project	Area	Area of Change in Use	Relocation Area	Method of Estimation
Factories	40	40	Farmland	As for farmland
Commercial	30	20	Farmland	As for farmland
Roads	40	–	–	–
Housing	30	20	Farmland	As for farmland
Government	10	0	0	Cost difference
Recreation	5	5	0	Willingness to pay
Farmland	20	20	0	Production forgone

– = not applicable.
Source: ADB Economic Research and Regional Cooperation Department.

6.   These different types of land use can be discussed in turn.
   a.   Factories will be relocated using the same amount of land, displacing agricultural production. There may be efficiency improvements for the factories, but the economic price of the land is the agricultural production forgone.
   b.   Commercial enterprises and housing will be relocated. However, the newly designed buildings will be more compact than the structures that

will be displaced, and so less land is reassigned at the relocation site. The economic price of the land is given through lost agricultural production.

c.   Existing roads will be widened as part of the new road and, hence, there is no change in land use for the existing road area.

d.   Some government offices will be displaced. They will not be replaced. Existing functions will be fitted into existing government premises nearby, entailing no further loss of land. The cost of the associated land can be estimated through the cost difference in providing government services. This cost difference may be negative, that is, the cost of providing services may be lower after displacement than before.

e.   A small amount of recreational area will be lost. It can be valued through an estimate of willingness to pay where no revenues are collected for the recreational services that are being lost.

f.   Finally, the farmland, and the associated agricultural production that is lost directly as a result of the road, will not be compensated elsewhere.

7.   The economic price of land for the different effects of changes in land use should be measured in or converted to economic prices. Where the economic price is estimated through the annual lost production in agricultural or other activities, this is usually included in the project statement for each year. Where the economic price is estimated through an adjusted purchase or lease price, this will be included as a single payment in the first project year.

B.   Treatment of Resettlement

8.   The costs of resettlement should be included in the project financial and economic costs, in addition to land. Projects with no change in land use are likely to involve no resettlement. For many, the resettlement of population and economic activities will be small, but for some, it may constitute a significant proportion of the project costs. ADB requires that the involuntary resettlement of populations be treated as an integral part of project design.[1]

9.   The financial costs of resettlement may include
a.   compensation for lost income for a specified period,
b.   compensation for the loss of assets or the reconstruction costs of housing and workshops,
c.   compensation for temporary production losses during relocation,
d.   the cost of relocation, and
e.   the cost of managing the resettlement process.

[1]   ADB. 1998. *Handbook on Resettlement: A Guide to Good Practice*. https://www.adb.org/sites/default/files/institutional-document/32259/handbook-resettlement.pdf

10.   Compensation for lost income for a specified period is a transfer payment and reflects the opportunity cost of lost production from the land and should be excluded from the costs of resettlement where the economic price of land has already been estimated. Otherwise, the loss of income from the land will be included twice. Other forms of compensation payment need to be substituted by the actual costs of removal and reconstruction. All resource costs involved in resettlement, such as the cost of rehousing, should be valued at economic prices.

Appendix 10:
Depletion Premium

1.　Many projects involve exploitation of depletable resources, either as an input or an output. The key characteristic of a depletable resource is that its use leads to a decline in its stock—either the stock is fixed or the rate of use exceeds the rate of replenishment. Normally, mineral and energy deposits are treated as depletable resources. However, environmental goods, such as wilderness, topsoil, ozone layers, water aquifers, and endangered species, are also depletable resources. Economic analysis of projects needs to explicitly include the economic cost of depletion.

2.　Depletable resources could be either tradable or non-tradable goods. Most energy and mineral goods are tradables, whereas most environmental goods are non-tradable. Valuation of depletable resources requires the inclusion of an explicit opportunity cost component for depletion, in addition to the marginal extraction costs. This opportunity cost is often referred to as a depletion premium. The depletion premium is an additional amount equivalent to the present value of the economic cost of extracting the resource at some time in the future, over and above its economic price today.

3.　In general, the depletion premium (DP) for a particular year can be defined as

$$DP_t = \frac{(PS_T - CS_t)(1+r)^t}{(1+r)^T} \qquad (1)$$

where DP_t = depletion premium at time t;
　　　PST = price of substitute at the time of complete exhaustion T;
　　　CS_t = extraction cost of present resource;
　　　r　 = discount rate; and
　　　T　 = time of exhaustion of deposit.

4.　This means that DP is given by the cost per unit of the replacement resource at the time of exhaustion (PS_T) minus the saving in extraction cost (CS_t). Two cases of depletion premium are encountered:
　　a.　with no stock effect, where the cost of extraction is independent of the remaining stock; and
　　b.　with stock effect, where the cost of extraction depends on the remaining stock level.

5.   In most projects, the assumption of constant marginal extraction cost is used and that is what is illustrated below. All values are economic values at constant prices, so it is assumed that both replacement and extraction cost are constant in real terms.

Depletion Premium without Stock Effects: Natural Gas Illustration

6.   Natural gas is a depletable resource and many countries have finite stocks. Consider a project that requires natural gas as an input. The calculation of a depletion premium for natural gas requires the basic data outlined in Table A10. Then using equation (1), assuming the price of the fuel substitute in year 15 to be $4.50/million British thermal unit; using 9% as a discount rate; and taking 2015 as the base year for calculations (t = 0), we have

$$\text{Depletion Premium (2015)} = (4.5 - 0.75) \times (1.09)0 / (1.09)^{15}$$
$$= 1.03$$

$$\text{Depletion Premium (2016)} = (4.5 - 0.75) \times (1.09)1 / (1.09)^{15}$$
$$= 1.12$$

and so on. The depletion premium increases as the stock diminishes. For the price to reflect depletion, the project economic analysis will include the economic cost of $0.75 (which is the present unit extraction cost) plus the opportunity cost of depletion of $1.03 in 2015, and $0.75 plus the depletion premium of $1.12 in 2016, and so on. The economic value of the natural gas input, therefore, increases over time until the stock is exhausted. By year 15, the depletion premium will be $3.75 and the full cost of gas will be its price of $4.50.

Table A10: Depletion Premium for Natural Gas: Data

Data Required	
Size of deposits	11.0 tcf
Extraction rate	750 bcf
Life of deposit/years to exhaustion	15 years
Present extraction costs (LRMC)	$0.75/mmbtu
Substitute fuel	fuel oil
Present price of substitute fuel	$2.25/mmbtu
Price of substitute fuel oil at exhaustion	$4.50/mmbtu
Discount rate used	9%

bcf = billion cubic feet, LRMC = long-run marginal cost, mmbtu = million British thermal unit, tcf = trillion cubic feet.
Source: ADB Economic Research and Regional Cooperation Department.

Appendix 11:
Use of Domestic Price Numeraire

1.   In many economies, transaction costs, taxes, and nontariff barriers raise domestic market price levels higher than world market price levels. Where some project outputs and inputs are valued at world market prices and others at domestic market prices, there is a need to bring all values to a common base so that they can be aggregated into an estimate of project net benefits. This common base can be the domestic price level (domestic price numeraire) or world price level (world price numeraire). In both cases, the analysis can use a national currency or a foreign currency. Whichever option is chosen, the analysis will lead to the same investment decision. This appendix illustrates how to apply the domestic price numeraire approach.

2.   When using the domestic price numeraire, all project outputs and inputs are valued at the domestic price level in national currency. This means converting all world market prices in foreign currency into the national currency using the official exchange rate, and to further adjust this to the domestic price level using a shadow exchange rate factor (SERF). Since SERF is the ratio of the shadow exchange rate (SER) to official exchange rate, the world price values in foreign currency can also be converted directly into domestic price values in national currency using the SER.

3.   Table A11.1 illustrates an example of applying these adjustments. A project will produce certain quantities of rice that will substitute for imported rice. At the official exchange rate of Rs10 per $1, the total financial value of the project's rice output amounting to Rs400 can be broken down as in column 3 of Table A11.1. A SER of Rs12.50 per $1 has been estimated for the country concerned, implying a SERF of 1.25. Using the domestic price numeraire, the SERF is applied to the traded goods component of the imported rice that will be substituted; handling, transport, and nontraded components are not adjusted since they are at domestic prices. No indirectly traded content can be identified, and taxes on the imported rice are excluded. So the economic value of the rice at the domestic price level in national currency is Rs425.

Table A11.1: Deriving Economic Value Using Domestic Price Numeraire

	Conversion Factor	Financial Value in National Currency	Economic Value at Domestic Prices in National Currency
Import price/traded component	1.25	300	375
Handling and transport/nontraded component	1.00	50	50
Import duties and excise taxes	0.00	50	0
Total value	–	400	425

– = not applicable.
Notes:
1. SERF = 1.25, SER = Rs12.50.
2. Economic value at domestic prices in national currency: Rs375 + Rs50 = Rs425
Source: ADB Economic Research and Regional Cooperation Department.

4.   The following railway project provides another example. Table A11.2 disaggregates project inputs and outputs into their traded and nontraded goods components. On the input side, the civil work element of capital costs involves both traded and nontraded goods components. All machinery and equipment is treated as traded goods wherever it is purchased. The opportunity cost of land is measured in traded goods while resettlement costs are treated as nontraded.[1]   For operating costs, the opportunity cost of surplus labor is estimated in traded goods, while administrative expenses are treated as nontraded goods.[2]

Table A11.2: Structure of Railway Project Costs and Benefits

Project Costs	National Currency (CNY million)		
	Traded Goods World Prices	Nontraded Goods Domestic Prices	Total
Capital Costs			
Civil works	720.0	1,360.0	2,080.0
Machinery and equipment	336.0	0.0	336.0
Land and resettlement	0.0	320.0	320.0
Consultant services	24.0	16.0	40.0
Total Capital Costs	**1,080.0**	**1,696.0**	**2,776.0**
Operating Costs			
Fuel	32.0	0.0	32.0

continued on next page

[1]   Land is valued at lost output, which is taken to be in traded goods. In addition, there are resettlement costs that are taken to be nontraded costs (construction, labor, etc.). The two are reported under nontraded goods as land is nontraded.
[2]   For simplicity, it is assumed that there are no taxes in any of the values in Table A11.2.

Table A11.2. continued

	National Currency (CNY million)		
Labor (surplus)	25.0	0.0	25.0
Labor (scarce)	0.0	28.0	28.0
Other	0.0	56.0	56.0
Total Operating Costs	**57.0**	**84.0**	**141.0**
Project Benefits			
Avoided road transport costs	0.0	280.0	280.0
Additional net output	240.0	0.0	240.0
Total	240.0	280.0	520.0
Memo Items			
Official Exchange Rate			
(CNY/$)		8.00	
Shadow Exchange Rate			
Factor		1.08	
Discount Rate		9%	

Source: ADB Economic Research and Regional Cooperation Department.

5. On the output side, there are two forms of project output: avoided road transport costs and extra net output achieved through releasing congestion on the system. The latter is estimated directly in traded goods. The opportunity cost of scarce labor and the avoided road transport costs, in principle, represent a mixture of traded and nontraded goods. However, in practice, they are often not separated. Here, they are treated as nontraded components.

6. Table A11.2 presents project costs and benefits in domestic currency or yuan. The official exchange rate is taken as CNY8 to $1 and all the figures could equally have been expressed in US dollars by multiplication by 8.0. A SERF of 1.08 has also been estimated, implying that the domestic prices in which the nontraded components are estimated on average are 8% higher than the world price equivalents in which the traded good components are estimated. Table A11.3 presents the project economic statement in national currency at the domestic price level, by applying the SERF to the value of all the traded goods components (the latter are shown in Table A11.2).

Table A11.3: Project Economic Statement, National Currency, and Domestic Price Level

Project Costs	Present Value	Years			
		0	1	2	3–25
Capital Costs					
Civil works		2,138			
Machinery and equipment		363			
Land and resettlement		320			
Consultant services		42			
Total Capital Costs	2,627	2,863	0	0	0
Operating Costs					
Fuel			35	35	35
Labor (surplus)			27	27	27
Labor (scarce)			28	28	28
Other			56	56	56
Total Operating Costs	1,316	0	146	146	146
Project Benefits					
Avoided road transport costs			280	280	280
Additional net output			259	259	259
Total	4,857	0	539	539	539
Net Benefits	914.9	(2,863)	393	393	393
EIRR (%)	13.1				

( ) = negative, EIRR = economic internal rate of return.
Note: From Years 3–25, operating costs and its components as well as project benefits and its components are assumed to remain constant.
Source: ADB Economic Research and Regional Cooperation Department.

Appendix 12:
Illustration of Estimating
the Shadow Exchange Rate

1.   The shadow exchange rate (SER) is the economic price of foreign currency. Even with a floating exchange system, where the rate is determined by the market, there is no guarantee that the SER is equal to the market or official exchange rate (OER). That would be the case only if there were no taxes and subsidies on the demand and supply of tradable goods, and the present exchange rate reflected the long-run equilibrium value of foreign currency over the life of a project.

2.   Exchange rates are one of the key macro prices affecting project performance. If the OER is overvalued (so the price of a unit of local currency relative to foreign currency is above its long-run equilibrium level), then projects producing non-tradables are favored relative to projects producing tradables. On the other hand, if the OER is undervalued (so the price of local currency is too low), projects producing tradables are favored relative to projects producing non-tradables.

A.   Shadow Exchange Rate Factor

3.   In theory, the SER should reflect the welfare change created by the availability of an additional unit of foreign exchange (in the case of a project that generates additional supply of foreign exchange) or by the use of an additional unit of foreign exchange (in the case of a project that generates a demand for foreign exchange) or by a combination of the two effects. The shadow exchange rate factor (SERF) is the ratio of the SER to the OER, with both the SER and the OER expressed in the same base year prices used for the project calculations.

4.   In principle, the value of the SER should be estimated for each year of a project's life and applied to the traded components of annual benefits and costs, although it is often adequate to use a single SERF for all the years, on the assumption that the ratio of the SER to the OER is unchanged over the life of a project.[1]

5.   Under a set of restrictive conditions, domestic market prices can be used to approximate the value of goods made available through additional imports or diverted from domestic use as additional exports as a result of a project. This allows a weighted

---

[1]   If a world price numeraire is to be applied, a standard conversion factor (SCF) can be used and is calculated as the inverse of the SERF. All procedures for estimation discussed here therefore apply equally to the SCF. It should be noted that while use of the SCF as a form of indirect exchange rate is a shortcut approximation to what was originally intended in the application of the world price numeraire.

average of the ratio of domestic to world prices for traded goods to approximate the SER. With taxes and subsidies on trade taken to determine the difference between domestic and world prices, this leads to a formula for the SER as

$$SER = OER \times (\Sigma w_m \times (1 + t_m - s_m) + \Sigma w_x \times (1 - t_x + s_x)) \tag{1}$$

6.   Where m and x are individual import and export products respectively; OER is the prevailing official exchange rate (in units of local currency per unit of foreign currency); t_m and t_x are rates of tax on imports m and exports x, respectively, s_m and s_x are rates of subsidy on m and x; and w_m and w_x are the weights placed on m and x. Summation Σ covers all imports and all exports. The signs on taxes and subsidies are opposite since import taxes raise domestic prices above world levels and import subsidies reduce them below world levels. Similarly, relative to world market levels, export taxes reduce domestic prices and export subsidies raise them. Where quota restrictions are in force, in principle this requires information on the tariff equivalent price effect of a quota. In practice, given World Trade Organization regulations, such restrictions are now much less common and this component of the formula is usually ignored on the assumption that it will not be significant.

7.   In theory, where a project's effect is large enough to change the OER, the shares of different imports and exports in (1) will be determined by the size of the import elasticities of demand for individual imports m and the export elasticities of supply for individual exports x, and the share of m and x in total trade. Where m refers to all imports and x to all exports, η is the negative import price elasticity of demand and ε is the export elasticity of supply, M is the total value of imports, and X is the total value of exports, the weights are $w_m = -\eta \times (M/X) / (\varepsilon - \eta \times (M/X))$ and $w_x = \varepsilon / (\varepsilon - \eta \times (M/X))$.[2]

8.   Where detailed information on trade elasticities is not available, a common simplifying assumption is that all elasticities are equal to 1.0, so that existing average shares in foreign trade equal marginal shares in new trade created by a project. This means that where M and X refer to total trade, the weight w_m will be $M/(M + X)$ and the weight w_x will be $X/(M + X)$. This simplification allows (1) to be approximated by a commonly used short cut expression for the SERF:

$$SERF = ((M + T_m - S_m) + (X - T_x + S_x)) / (M + X) \tag{2}$$

---

[2]   Where foreign exchange for a project is obtained from the capital market or borrowed from abroad, the analysis is more complicated and effects on nontraded activities also have to be allowed for.

9.   Where M and X are the total value of imports and exports, respectively, in foreign currency converted to domestic currency at the OER, and T_m and T_x are total taxes on imports and exports, respectively, and S_m and S_x are the total subsidies on imports and exports, respectively.

10.   Equations (1) and (2) make the SER and SERF dependent solely on trade taxes and subsidies. This is a common adjustment in practical appraisal, but even accepting its assumptions on domestic prices, it is only correct where the OER reflects the underlying or equilibrium real exchange rate (EER) over the life of a project. In theory, like any other relative price change, a change in the underlying real value of foreign exchange, which operates over the life of a project, should be incorporated in an appraisal.

11.   Therefore, where the real exchange rate prevailing at the time of appraisal does not reflect the underlying real value of foreign exchange at the prices of the base year, this should be incorporated in the formula for the SER. Where an estimate is available for the EER, the formula for the SER needs to be modified by introducing an additional premium (where EER > OER) or discount (where EER < OER). Thus, where EER/OER = p, the SER formula (1) becomes

$$SER = p \times OER \times (\Sigma w_m \times (1 + t_m - s_m) + \Sigma w_x \times (1 - t_x + s_x)) \tag{3}$$

Or $$SER = EER \times (\Sigma w_m \times (1 + t_m - s_m) + \Sigma w_x \times (1 - t_x + s_x))$$

Similarly (2) becomes

$$SERF = p \times ((M + T_m - S_m) + (X - T_x + S_x)) / (M + X) \tag{4}$$

12.   Estimating the underlying or equilibrium exchange rate can be complex since it can be defined as the rate that achieves external balance or as the rate that achieves both internal as well as external balance. An approximate approach, which focuses only on the external balance, defines the equilibrium rate as one that creates a sustainable level for the current account balance, which is a deficit that can be financed by long-run capital inflows or a current account surplus that corresponds to desired long-run capital outflows. For purposes of illustration, it is assumed that current account imbalance of 3% of gross domestic product (GDP), either surplus or deficit, is assumed to be sustainable.

13.   Where the EER is defined in this way, it can be estimated from trade elasticities and a judgment on the sustainable trade deficit.[3] Where products m and x refer to total imports and exports, and M and X give their total value, the trade deficit D will be $M - X$. If d is the proportion of the deficit, which is sustainable, the exchange rate, which removes the deficit (EER), is given as

$$EER = OER \times (1 + \{(1-d) \times D / (\varepsilon \times X - \eta \times M)\}) \qquad (5)$$

where ε and η are the elasticities of export supply and import demand, respectively. On the assumptions that foreign demand is perfectly elastic and that a country's own trade elasticities are constant, $(\varepsilon \times X - \eta \times M)/100$ gives the change in the trade deficit caused by 1% change in the exchange rate (holding domestic prices constant). As d is the proportion of the deficit that is sustainable $(1-d) \times D$ gives the value of the deficit that needs to be reduced. The ratio $(1-d) \times D$ to the change in the trade balance induced by a 1% change in the exchange rate gives the percentage adjustment needed to bring the deficit to a sustainable level of $d \times D$.[4]

B.   Shadow Exchange Rate for the Philippines: An Example

14.   The analysis is conducted for the Philippines' SER relative to the US dollar. The basic SER is estimated based on data on trade taxes. These are import duties, value-added tax (VAT), and excise duties. It appears that exports are not taxed and no subsidies on trade are reported (so t_x, s_m, and s_x are zero). Table A12 gives data on total imports, exports, and taxes on trade 2010–2014. Elasticity estimates for total exports and imports for the Philippines are taken from a secondary source and are used for estimating as weights in the SER estimate.[5]

15.   The basic SER equation for 2014 based on taxes on trade gives an SER of P48.30/$1.00 and a SERF of 1.09. The average over the period 2010–2014 is similar, with an SER of P46.61/$1.00 and a SERF of 1.07. Over the period, there is a trade deficit with imports exceeding exports by an average 7% of GDP annually.

---

[3]   Other approaches to the equilibrium exchange rate are possible. One follows a modified version of the purchasing power parity theory of exchange rate determination, which implies that exchange rates move in line with inflation differentials and that in the very long run, prices in different economies will converge. Another approach estimates the equilibrium exchange rate econometrically as the rate that generates both external balance (a current account fundable by sustained long-run capital flows) and internal balance (where potential and actual output are equal).

[4]   Dividing both sides of the ratio $\{(1-d) \times D / (\varepsilon \times X - \eta \times M)\}$ by 100 gives the proportionate change in the exchange rate required to reduce $(1-d) \times D$ to zero.

[5]   S. Tokarick. 2010. *A method for calculating export supply and import demand elasticities.* IMF Working Paper 10/180. IMF.

This is more than offset by remittances and other current account flows, so that over the same period there is a current account surplus in each year averaging around 4% of GDP.

Table A12: Trade Data for the Philippines and the Shadow Exchange Rate Factor

Item	Variable/ Equation	Value for 2014 ($ million)	Average Value for 2010–2014 ($ million)
Total Exports	X	47,758	42,741
Total Imports	M	63,609	60,686
Trade Balance	D	(15,851)	(17,945)
Trade taxes			
Exports	T_x	0	
Imports	Tm	9,192	
Rate of import tax	$t_m = T_m/M$	0.144	0.115
Rate of export tax	$t_x = T_x/X$	0	0
Elasticity of export supply	ε	2.04	2.04
Elasticity of import demand	η	(2.32)	(2.32)
Weight on exports	$w_x = \varepsilon/(\varepsilon - \eta \times (M/X))$	0.398	0.382
Weight on imports	$w_m = (-\eta \times (M/X))/(\varepsilon - \eta \times (M/X))$	0.602	0.618
Official exchange rate	OER	P44.40/$	P43.50/$
Alternative 1: When the current account is sustainable			
SER1	$SER = OER \times (\Sigma w_m \times (1 + t_m) + \Sigma w_x \times (1 - t_x))$	P48.26/$	P46.61/$
SERF1	SER/OER	1.087	1.071
Alternative 2: When the current account is unsustainable			
Exchange rate to remove all trade deficit	$EER = ER \times (1 + \{D/(\varepsilon \times X - \eta \times M)\})$	$EER = OER \times (1.06) =$ P47.27/$	$EER = OER \times (1.08) =$ P46.92/$
Real exchange rate misalignment	p = EER/OER	p = 47.27/44.40= 1.06	p = 46.92/43.50 = 1.08
SER2	$SER = p \times OER \times (\Sigma w_m \times (1 + t_m) + \Sigma w_x \times (1 - t_x))$	$SER = 1.06 \times 48.26 =$ 51.38	$SER = 1.08 \times 46.61 =$ 50.28
SERF2	SER/OER	SERF = 51.38/44.40 = 1.16	SERF = 50.28/43.50 = 1.16

EER= equilibrium exchange rate, OER = official exchange rate, P = Philippine peso, SER = shadow exchange rate, SERF = shadow exchange rate factor.
Source: ADB Economic Research and Regional Cooperation Department.

16.   If the remittances and other current account flows are sustainable, this suggests that there is little misalignment of the real exchange rate and little undervaluation of foreign currency (as SER1 is close to OER). However, if remittances and other flows are transitory rather than stable and will decline in the future, an exchange rate adjustment will be needed to reduce the trade deficit. To illustrate the approach, an equilibrium exchange rate (EER) required to remove the trade deficit based on aggregate trade elasticities and the current level of protection on trade is estimated at P47/$1.00, with the rate approximately the same for 2014 alone and for the period 2010–2014. When this EER is combined with the data on trade taxes, a revised shadow exchange rate and conversion factor (SER2 and SERF2) are obtained. For 2014, the SER2 is P51.4 and the SERF2 is 1.16. The results are similar for the period 2010–2014.

17.   The premium on foreign exchange implied by this analysis is around 8% if the exchange rate is not fundamentally misaligned. Incorporating an approximate exchange rate adjustment adds another 8 percentage points to give a revised premium of 16%. As the resulting SERF is considerably higher with the exchange rate adjustment, it is desirable that its realism be tested by reference to other estimates.

Appendix 13:
Using Conversion Factors:
A Water Project Example

1.   A project supplies water to an area previously suffering from intermittent connections and poor water quality. It is assumed that total water usage per household will remain unchanged with the project, but a survey has revealed that households on average are willing to pay a 15% premium above the normal tariff to obtain higher quality service. Costs of the project include capital cost divided between imported equipment (40%) and local construction cost (60%), and operating cost divided between wages (30%), fuel (30%), and local parts and components (40%). There is a 2-year construction period and a 10-year operating life. The project statement at financial prices is in Table A13.1 with water valued at the national tariff. The return on the project is a financial internal rate of return of 13% and there is a financial net present value at 9% of $19.03 million.

Table A13.1: Water Project Data in Financial Prices
(million)

								Years				
		0	1	2	3	4	5	6	7	8	9	10	11
Water Revenues		0	0	90	110	110	110	110	110	110	110	110	110
Capital Cost													
Equipment		20	40										
Construction		30	60										
Operating Cost													
Wages				25	25	25	25	25	25	25	25	25	25
Fuel				20	25	25	25	25	25	25	25	25	25
Materials				33.3	40	40	40	40	40	40	40	40	40
Total cost		50	100	78.3	90	90	90	90	90	90	90	90	90
Net		(50)	(100)	11.7	20	20	20	20	20	20	20	20	20
NPV at 9%	19.03												
FIRR	13%												

( ) = negative, FIRR = financial internal rate of return, NPV = net present value.
Source: ADB Economic Research and Regional Cooperation Department.

2. For the economic valuation, a number of adjustments are to be made.
    a. Willingness to pay for water is introduced with a premium of 15%.
    b. All taxes on cost are excluded.
    c. Surplus labor is employed in building the project, and labor costs in construction are adjusted by a conversion factor (CF) of 0.70 (implying opportunity costs are 70% of the wage paid).
    d. The exchange rate is estimated to be overvalued by 15% (SERF = 1.15).

3. To introduce these adjustments, first the benefits and costs of the project at financial prices are disaggregated into traded and nontraded items, surplus and scarce labor, and transfers using a set of estimated coefficients. For the economic valuation, based on willingness to pay, the economic value of water is taken as 15% above the tariff. An analysis of cost data suggests that the equipment component of capital cost is composed of 90% cost, insurance, and freight price, 4.5% import duty, and 5.5% cost of local transport to the project, which is treated as a nontraded cost. The cost of construction is composed of 40% surplus labor, 10% scarce labor, 30% nontraded materials, 10% imported traded materials, and 10% taxes. Estimates of operating costs suggest all labor is scarce (that is, it has other employment opportunities), fuel is 80% traded and 20% indirect taxes, and local parts and components are 80% nontraded and 20% taxes. All nontraded project costs are included under the nontraded cost category. This information is summarized in Table A13.2.

4. The financial price data are disaggregated into the resource categories by applying the shares from Table A13.2 to the project information in Table A13.1 to give the resource flows by category in Table A13.3. For example, cost of traded goods in year 0 is equal to 0.9 × 20+0.1 × 30 (i.e., sum of the share of traded goods in equipment cost in year 0 and share of traded goods in construction cost in year 0).[1] Economic analysis then requires the application of CFs to these different categories as set out in Table A13.4.

---

[1] While a part of fuel costs is traded, there is no fuel cost incurred in year 0. Fuel costs are incurred beginning year 2.

Table A13.2: Cost and Benefit Breakdown
(in percentage distribution)

	Benefits – Nontraded (Willingness to Pay)	Costs – Traded	Costs – Nontraded	Scarce Labor	Surplus Labor	Transfers	Total
Water	100						100
Capital Cost							
Equipment		90	5.5			4.5	100
Construction		10	30	10	40	10	100
Operating Cost							
Labor				100			100
Fuel		80				20	100
Parts and Components			80			20	100

Source: ADB Economic Research and Regional Cooperation Department.

Table A13.3: Disaggregation by Category
(Financial Prices)

Benefits						Years						
	0	1	2	3	4	5	6	7	8	9	10	11
Traded	0	0	0	0	0	0	0	0	0	0	0	0
Willingness to pay for nontraded output	0	0	103.5	126.5	126.5	126.5	126.5	126.5	126.5	126.5	126.5	126.5
Transfers	0	0	(13.5)	(16.5)	(16.5)	(16.5)	(16.)5	(16.5)	(16.5)	(16.5)	(16.5)	(16.5)
Costs												
Traded	21	42	16	20	20	20	20	20	20	20	20	20
Nontraded	10.1	20.2	26.64	32	32	32	32	32	32	32	32	32
Scarce labor	3	6	25	25	25	25	25	25	25	25	25	25
Surplus labor	12	24	0	0	0	0	0	0	0	0	0	0
Transfers	3.9	7.8	10.66	13	13	13	13	13	13	13	13	13
Total	**50**	**100**	**78.3**	**90**	**90**	**90**	**90**	**90**	**90**	**90**	**90**	**90**

( ) = negative.
Source: ADB Economic Research and Regional Cooperation Department.

Table A13.4: Conversion Factors of Major Resource Categories

Resource Category	Conversion Factor
Traded	1.15
Willingness to pay – Nontraded output	1.15
Nontraded cost	1.0
Scarce labor	1.0
Surplus labor	0.7
Transfers	0

Source: ADB Economic Research and Regional Cooperation Department.

5.   This gives the cost–benefit stream in economic prices, which is set out in Table A13.5. For example, the benefits in willingness to pay in year 3 are 90 (the financial price data) multiplied by 1.15 to give 103.5; similarly, surplus labor costs in year 1 are the wages of 12 multiplied by 0.7 to give 8.4. Nontraded costs and skilled labor costs are the same in financial and economic prices, while transfers are multiplied by zero and, therefore, are removed from the economic analysis. The result is an economic internal rate of return of 26% and an economic net present value at 9% of $122.38 million. All the economic adjustments (apart from the increase in traded costs due to the exchange rate adjustment) make the project look better than in the financial analysis, but the main change is through the introduction of a willingness-to-pay value for water.

6.   Highlighting and adjusting the categories in this way allow the analysis to focus on what are likely to be the key economic valuation issues for most projects—the extent to which consumers are willing to pay more for project outputs relative to what they are asked to pay, the taxes and subsidies involved with the project, the project's use of foreign exchange, and the extent to which the exchange rate is misaligned, and any significant employment effects. The conversion factors can be altered as necessary to test the sensitivity of the project to what is assumed about the key variables, particularly willingness to pay for output and the exchange rate.

Table A13.5: Economic Cost and Benefit in Domestic Prices
(million)

Economic Valuation	0	1	2	3	4	5	6	7	8	9	10	11
Benefits												
Willingness to pay – Nontraded output	0	0	103.5	126.5	126.5	126.5	126.5	126.5	126.5	126.5	126.5	126.5
Costs												
Traded	24.15	48.3	18.4	23	23	23	23	23	23	23	23	23
Nontraded	10.1	20.2	26.64	32	32	32	32	32	32	32	32	32
Scarce labor	3	6	25	25	25	25	25	25	25	25	25	25
Surplus labor	8.4	16.8	0	0	0	0	0	0	0	0	0	0
Transfers	0	0	0	0	0	0	0	0	0	0	0	0
Total costs	45.65	91.3	70.04	80	80	80	80	80	80	80	80	80
Net Benefits	**(45.65)**	**(91.3)**	**33.46**	**46.5**	**46.5**	**46.5**	**46.5**	**46.5**	**46.5**	**46.5**	**46.5**	**46.5**
ENPV	122.38											
EIRR	26%											

( ) = negative, EIRR = economic internal rate of return, ENPV = economic net present value.
Note: Conversion factor for traded is1.15, nontraded is1.0, scarce labor is 1.0, surplus labor is 0.7, and transfers is 0.
Source: ADB Economic Research and Regional Cooperation Department.

Appendix 14:
Examples of Benefit Transfer Method

A.   Unit Value Transfer

1.   A project to rehabilitate coral reefs will create benefits by reducing beach erosion as the reefs act as a barrier to strong tides and waves. For example, an erosion control value of coral reefs has been estimated in area X at $400/hectare. If the coastline involved in area X is sufficiently similar to that associated with the project, a simple version of benefit transfer adjusts this value to the prices of the project's base year using an index of international inflation. If the original estimate is for 2005, the base year is 2012, and international inflation is 2% annually, this gives a 2012 value of $459/hectare.[1] This approximate value for the erosion control of coral reefs can be applied to the area of reefs at risk, which the project will protect.

B.   Benefit Function Transfer

2.   Where the benefit to be transferred is a willingness-to-pay figure and there are significant differences between income level in the country of the reference study and the country in which the project under consideration is located, a simple approach is to scale for these income differences.[2] A more sophisticated means of addressing differences between project conditions and those of the reference study is a benefit function transfer, which involves transferring a functional relationship rather than a value between one location and another. The benefit function transfer approach can be applied where a contingent valuation survey is used to estimate household willingness to pay to protect the environment. The results of a survey of respondents in one administrative area (A) can be used to derive willingness-to-pay estimates for households in a different area (B). Respondents in area A are asked if they would be willing to pay a unique bid price to remove pollution from a river basin. Data are also collected on a set of explanatory variables, which are likely to influence their willingness to pay. Among others, explanatory variables include monthly household income, age of head of household (years), gender of head of

---

[1]   The cumulative price rise is approximately 15% as $(1.02)^7 = 0.1486$.

[2]   Estimates of economic values are known to depend on level of income, then it is occasionally possible to proceed with transfer while adjusting for possible differences in the levels of income. The adjustment is made as follows: $B_p = B_E (Y_p / Y_E)^e$. BP stands for the estimated benefit for the site impacted by the project; BE is the estimated benefits in existing studies; Y_p and Y_E are income per capita for the population impacted by the project and the population in existing studies, respectively; and e is the income elasticity of the benefits assumed to be the same in both countries. If it is assumed that income elasticity is equal to 1, then the adjustment in the economic values is simply in proportion of the differences in per capita income.

household (male being 1), education of head (years of schooling), distance from river (in kilometers), and pollution intensity in area (index number).

3. A Probit model explaining the yes/no response to a given price and using the set of explanatory variables has already been estimated for area A. The benefit function transfer approach applies the relationship between willingness to pay and the bid price and the explanatory variables (for example, the link between willingness to pay and income) found for area A to the relevant data on the same set of explanatory variables, reflecting the characteristics of area B.

4. Table A14 shows the estimated coefficients based on data from the survey in area A and the respective means of the variables and the mean values of the explanatory variables for area B. In area A, the willingness to pay to remove river pollution is negatively related to charge imposed and as expected is positively related to income and the level of pollution and negatively related to distance from the river.

5. The coefficients estimated for area A are multiplied by the means of the explanatory variables for area B. The sum of the products of the coefficients and the means plus the constant (8.10) is then divided by the absolute value of the bid coefficient (–0.19) derived for area A. The result is multiplied by –1 to give a positive number. The estimated mean willingness to pay for B is 42.62 per household per month, which is about 10% lower than the figure of 47.38 per month for area A, with the difference mainly attributable to the difference in income between the two areas. Economic benefits are then estimated by multiplying the mean willingness to pay by the number of households affected.

Table A14: Benefit Function Transfer Calculation

Variables	Coefficient for A	Mean A	Mean B	Coefficient A$_x$ Mean A	Coefficient A$_x$ Mean B
Bid price	(0.19)				
Household income	0.0003	24,502	21,302	7.3506	6.3906
Age of head	0.004	43.38	44.21	0.17352	0.17684
Gender	0.003	0.49	0.49	0.00147	0.00147
Distance from river	(0.003)	3.79	2.52	(0.01137)	(0.00756)
Pollution level	0.04	7.20	8.40	0.288	0.336
Constant	1.2			1.2	1.2
Total				**9.00222**	**8.09735**

( ) = negative.
Mean willingness to pay of A = (9.00222/(–0.19)) × (–1) = 47.380105
Mean willingness to pay of B = (8. 09735/(–0.19)) × (–1) = 42.61763
Source: ADB Economic Research and Regional Cooperation Department.

Appendix 15:
Distribution Analysis
of Regional Cooperation Projects

A.   Procedure

1.   Regional distribution analysis examines the distribution of benefits between countries emanating from regional cooperation projects. As in the national case, it is first necessary to establish who gains and who loses from the operation of the project valued at financial prices. As a first step, the financing structure of the project (its loan and equity mix) must be identified and income flows to equity investors and lenders estimated. Any project-specific finance with a concessional element, in the sense that capital inflows exceed outflows will be a benefit for the recipient country. Foreign capital inflows from outside the region are benefits when they are received and costs when they flow out as dividends or loan repayments.

2.   Next, it is necessary to consider how the externalities and price distortions associated with the project alter the allocation of income derived from the financial price calculations. Financial prices do not pick up the full effects of a project and some groups must gain where economic costs are below financial costs (for example, due to taxes) and where economic benefits are above financial benefits (for example, due to consumer surplus). Correspondingly, where financial costs are below economic costs (for example, due to a subsidy) and where financial benefits are above economic benefits (for example, due to import protection on output), some groups must lose. Hence, at this stage the analysis picks up the gainers and losers from externalities and price distortions in each country.

3.   The procedure involved can be summarized in five steps:

Step 1: Financial Return to Total Capital

Financial net present value (NPV) of the project at 9% should be calculated as a return to total capital before tax with all items valued at financial prices. Where the project has no marketed output, present value of costs alone should be given.

Step 2: Financial Flows from Financing Arrangements

The financial NPV at 9% going to different participants (equity investors, lenders, government) should be calculated. Groups from the region and outside can be identified and income gains for the latter should be excluded from the regional economic net present value (ENPV).

Step 3: Project-Specific Concessional Finance

Any public funds brought to the region specifically for this project should be identified. The difference between their inflow and outflow discounted at 9% gives an additional benefit created by the project, which must be added to the ENPV. The beneficiary of these funds should be identified. Note that this step relates only to additional public funds, since private foreign investment and loans are normally treated as project specific and are already included in Step 2.

Step 4: Economic Adjustments

Any externalities and market distortions must be allowed for by either multiplication by conversion factors or by adding extra benefit or cost figures. These adjustments reflect real income changes not measured by the financial NPV and must be allocated to different groups in the participating countries.

Step 5: Sensitivity Analysis

Sensitivity test can be applied as appropriate to check how changes in key variables affect both the total return and its distribution. A test for real exchange rate adjustments between the different countries is particularly appropriate for regional projects.

B.   Illustration: Power Export Project

4.   These steps are illustrated with a simple example: a power export project in a small country with sales to its larger neighbor. For ease of exposition, all data are given as present values at 9%, on the assumption that all relevant conversion factors (CFs) are constant. A zero rate of inflation is assumed to avoid the complication of converting nominal to real prices. Power produced in country B is predominantly exported to its neighbor country A.

Step 1: The financial NPV is calculated by comparing revenue from power sales with investment and operating costs at financial prices in constant US dollars. The financial NPV is $63.19 million (see Table A15.1).

Table A15.1: Financial Price Data
($ million, in constant prices)

Financial Analysis										
Years	1	2	3	4	5	6	7	8	9	10
Sales	0	0	72	108	108	108	108	108	108	108
Investment Cost										
Traded	87	118								
Nontraded	20	23								
Labor	8	8								
Transfer	4.35	5.9								
Operating Cost										
Traded	0	0	12.5	22.5	25	25	25	25	25	25
Nontraded	0	0	4	7.2	8	8	8	8	8	8
Labor	0	0	3	5.4	6	6	6	6	6	6
Transfer	0	0	1	1.8	2	2	2	2	2	2
Net	(119.35)	(154.9)	51.5	71.1	67	67	67	67	67	67
FIRR	15%									
FNPV	63.19									

( ) = negative, FIRR = financial internal rate of return, FNPV = financial net present value.
Note: Net = sales – investment cost – operating cost.
Source: ADB Economic Research and Regional Cooperation Department.

Step 2: The investors involved are a foreign investor from outside the region (FOR); the National Electricity Authority (NEA) in B who operates the project; and an investor (IP) from country A which is the importing country. The NEA holds 60% of the equity and the other two investors hold 20% each. Equity funds are 30% of the project cost and the rest is from debt finance. The lenders to the project are Asian Development Bank, suppliers of export credit, and a foreign commercial bank. Table A15.2 gives the phasing of the funding and the interest rates and repayment periods.

5.   The project creates a series of income flows from these arrangements, which affect regional distribution and which would not have occurred without the project. Taxes on profits are at a rate of 10% and there is also a royalty charge of 3% of sales.
   a.   NEA gains the difference between discounted after-tax profits on its equity stake and the discounted value of its equity investment (85.33 – 45.29 = 40.04 million).
   b.   FOR also gains the difference between discounted after-tax profits on its equity stake and the discounted value of its equity investment (28.44 – 15.09 = 13.35 million).

Table A15.2: Financing Structure

Equity 30%	Amount in Year 1 in $	Amount in Year 2 in $
NEA	49.365	
FOR	16.455	
IP	16.455	
Loan 70%		
Export Credit	0	38.395
Commercial	0	76.790
ADB	37.075	39.715

Loan terms	Amount in $	Interest rate	Period (years)
Export Credit	38.395	4%	5
Commercial	76.790	14%	4
ADB	76.790	2%	20

ADB = Asian Development Bank, FOR = foreign investor, IP = investor from importing country, NEA = National Electricity Authority.
Source: ADB Economic Research and Regional Cooperation Department.

c. Similarly, IP gains the difference between discounted after-tax profits on its equity stake and the discounted value of its equity investment (13.35 million).

d. The government of B where the project is located, gains the discounted value of profits tax on the project and royalty payments (10.27 + 14.26 = 24.53 million).[1]

e. Export creditors gain the difference between the discounted loan interest and principal repayments on the export credit and the discounted value of the loan inflow (26.82 − 30.61 = -3.79 million), and commercial creditors gain the difference between the discounted value of the loan interest and principal repayments and discounted value of the commercial loan (68.04 − 61.22 = 6.82 million respectively).[2]

6. The difference between the discounted repayments on the ADB loan (33.64 million) and its discounted value (64.76 million) is −31.12 million, which reflects the concessional terms of the loan. In financial terms, the gains to the other

---

[1] The taxes on capital and operating costs are added to government income at a later step when economic adjustments are made to the project data.
[2] Export credits are at a 4% interest rate; hence, when discounted at 12%, repayments of principal and interest are less than the loan.

parties associated with the project are due in part to this subsidy. The sum of these changes gives the present value at financial prices of the income change created by the project (see Table A15.3).

Table A15.3: Distribution of Net Income
(Present Values, Financial Prices)

Stakeholder	Amount in $
NEA	40.04
FOR	13.35
IP	13.35
Government	24.53
Export Credit	(3.79)
Commercial	6.82
ADB Loan	(31.12)
Total	63.19

( ) = negative, ADB = Asian Development Bank, FOR = foreign investor, IP = investor from importing country, NEA = National Electricity Authority.
Source: ADB Economic Research and Regional Cooperation Department.

7. However, not all of the income flows remain within the region and those that do not (or those that could be repatriated in the future) need to be excluded from the analysis. Of these changes, income flows to FOR and to export and commercial creditors ($13.35 + $6.82 – $3.79), which total 16.38 million are excluded from the ENPV as they are income that will go to extra-regional parties. This means that from the financial price analysis of the project, 46.81 million is income created for the region.

Step 3: Initially, it is assumed that none of the ADB funds are project specific in that they would have come to the country without the project. This means that none of the concessional element—measured as the difference between the present value of the loan inflows and the discounted value of service charge and repayment of principal and interest—is a regional benefit that goes to the government of B. This assumption is changed in the sensitivity analysis.

Step 4: The key CF used is for the sale of power since the financial charge at which power is exported from B to A is below the economic value of power in A (given by a combination of cost savings and willingness to pay), so financial revenue understates economic benefit to the region.

    a. The CF for power sales is 1.2, so 20% of revenue collected for power sales is treated as a consumer surplus. The difference between the economic value of power in A and financial revenue paid to B is a gain to the power sector in A, which goes to consumers in A (95.06 million).

b.   It is assumed that the SERF is unity in both countries, but the shadow wage rate factor is 0.8 in country B. This means that 20% of the wages paid on the project are gain to labor in B.

c.   All taxes on capital and operating costs of the project as transfers have no economic cost, but will go to the government of B.

d.   To calculate the ENPV and economic internal rate of return (EIRR), the CFs of 1.2 for sales, 0.8 for labor, and zero for transfers are applied to the respective categories.

8.   In addition, the project-specific investments that come to the region because of the project must be added as benefits when they are received and costs when they are repaid. The foreign investment from FOR, the export credit, and commercial loans are treated in this way. The foreign investment is a benefit when it is received and a cost when dividends are paid. Similarly, the loans are benefits when they are received and costs when interest and principal is repaid.

The ENPV giving total income gain to the region is now 167.08 million and the EIRR is 30% (see Table A15.4).

Table A15.4: Economic Analysis

Economic Analysis

Years	1	2	3	4	5	6	7	8	9	10
Sales	0	0	86.4	129.6	129.6	129.6	129.6	129.6	129.6	129.6
Investment Cost										
Traded	87	118								
Nontraded	20	23								
Labor	6.4	6.4								
Transfer	0	0								
Operating Cost										
Traded	0	0	12.5	22.5	25	25	25	25	25	25
Nontraded	0	0	4	7.2	8	8	8	8	8	8
Labor	0	0	2.4	4.32	4.8	4.8	4.8	4.8	4.8	4.8
Transfer	0	0	0	0	0	0	0	0	0	0
Net	(113.4)	(147.4)	67.5	95.58	91.8	91.8	91.8	91.8	91.8	91.8
Add: ADB Loan	0	0	0	0	0	0	0	0	0	0
Commercial	0.00	76.79	(29.95)	(27.61)	(24.57)	(21.89)				
Export Credit	0.00	38.40	(9.21)	(8.91)	(8.91)	(8.29)	(7.99)			
Investment	16.46	0.00	(1.98)	(5.85)	(5.60)	(5.92)	(10.29)	(11.89)	(11.89)	(3.47)
Net	(96.95)	(32.32)	26.36	53.56	52.72	55.71	73.91	79.91	79.91	95.27

ENPV	167.08
EIRR	30%

( ) = negative, ADB = Asian Development Bank, CF = conversion factor, EIRR = economic internal rate of return, ENPV = economic net present value.
Source: ADB Economic Research and Regional Cooperation Department.

9.   The full distribution of the gain to the region is shared between the two countries: 65% for A which is the importing country, and 35% for B which is the producing country (see Table A15.5). The first part of the table shows the income flows identified from the financial analysis and the second part shows the flows arising from the economic adjustments for CFs and the inclusion of part of the ADB loan. The ENPV of 167.08 million has been allocated between groups in the two countries. The main beneficiary group is composed of consumers in A who gain access to power at favorable tariff, which is below their willingness to pay. Consumers gain the difference between the present value of sales valued at willingness to pay and the present value of revenue actually paid. Workers gain the difference between the present value of wages paid and the present value of wages at the estimated shadow wage. The government gains the present value of taxes on both the investment and operating costs.

Table A15.5: Distribution Effect for the Region
(Present Values)

	Country A	Country B	Foreigners
Financial Gains			
NEA		40.04	
FOR			13.35
IP	13.35		
Government		24.53	
ADB loan		(31.12)	
Export credit			(3.79)
Commercial			6.82
Economic Gains			
Consumers	95.06		
Labor		7.86	
Government		17.36	
ADB loan		0.00	
Total	**108.41**	**58.67**	
%	**0.65**	**0.35**	

( ) = negative, ADB = Asian Development Bank, FOR = foreign investor, IP = investor from importing country, NEA = National Electricity Authority.
Source: ADB Economic Research and Regional Cooperation Department.

Step 5: The analysis is very sensitive to the assumption for the CF for power. If a CF of 1.05 is used, for example, the distribution of benefits between the two countries is reversed with over 60% of income gains now accruing to country B and the EIRR now 22%.

10.   The inclusion of a proportion of the ADB loan as a benefit is a matter of judgment. If 50% of the ADB loan is project specific, this means that 50% of the concessional element of 31.12 million, measured as the difference between the present value of the loan inflows and the present value of service charge and repayment of principal and interest (15.56 million) is a regional benefit, which goes to the government of B. With 50% of the loan treated in this way and the other base case assumptions retained, the ENPV rises to 182.64 million.

Appendix 16:
Estimating the Economic Rate of Return: Irrigation Rehabilitation Project

1.   A project to rehabilitate a supplemental wet season irrigation system covering 1,620,000 hectares of land has been proposed and costed. The main benefits from the rehabilitation would be an increase in the proportion of land that is irrigated, with corresponding increases in cropping intensity and yields, although the supplemental nature of the system means that it has no effect in the dry season, which still has too little water for cultivation. Also, the scheme at present requires a lot of maintenance work, so there would be some decline in operation and maintenance (O&M) costs with the project. The investment would take place over a 3-year period and the life of the scheme with normal maintenance has been estimated at 25 years. The total cost of the investment including construction activities and institutional support during implementation, is about Rs1,800 million. The annual O&M cost of the project is Rs7.92 million, but there is a net savings of operating costs relative to the without project situation of Rs10 million.

2.   Table A16.1 shows the expected impact on area, cropping intensity, and yields with and without the project. Irrigated areas are used to grow rice, and these areas will increase with rehabilitation. Unirrigated areas are used to grow vegetables for the local market, and these areas will decrease with rehabilitation. Taking all these factors into account, a substantial increase in rice production is expected from the irrigation scheme area, but an overall decline in vegetable production. While the project is being constructed, it is assumed that 10% of without project output of vegetables and a little more than this for rice will be forgone. For both rice and vegetable production, yield increases are expected to build up gradually to the with project levels of Table A16.1 in the third year after full implementation. In the first year after implementation, they are 50% of the full level, and in the second, they are 80%.

3.   The project investment and O&M costs, together with the agricultural inputs and outputs, have been estimated at financial prices. They need to be reexpressed in economic prices. A high shadow exchange rate factor of 1.33 due to a serious balance-of-payments problem has been estimated for the country. In the project area, a shadow wage rate factor at domestic prices for hired labor of 0.8 has been estimated. Economic project costs and benefits will be estimated in national currency at the domestic price level.

Table A16.1: Production With and Without the Project

Item	Unit	Without Project Irrigated	Without Project Unirrigated	With Project Irrigated	With Project Unirrigated	Increment Irrigated	Increment Unirrigated
Area	ha	99,000	63,000	135,000	27,000	36,000	(36,000)
Cropping intensity	%	72.2	61.1	100	72.2		
Yield, rice	mt/ ha	2.4		2.9			
Yield, vegetables	mt/ ha		5		6.5		
Production	mt	171,600	192,500	391,500	126,750	219,900	(65,750)

( ) = negative, ha = hectare, mt = metric ton.
Source: ADB Economic Research and Regional Cooperation Department.

4.   The farm-gate price of rice in the project area is Rs6,335 per metric ton. However, rice is imported into the country and the incremental rice as a result of the irrigation rehabilitation will substitute for imports. In economic prices, rice is valued at its cost, insurance, and freight price to the country, plus the additional costs of getting the rice to the project area where most of it will also be consumed. The cost breakdown of the border parity price of rice is 80% foreign currency and 20% of other nontraded costs in the country. This cost breakdown is given in Table A16.2.

5.   Table A16.2 also gives the cost breakdown of the financial price values of the other project outputs and inputs. The vegetables are grown and sold in the project area; they are not of sufficient quality to be considered for export or to substitute for imports. Other agricultural inputs are nontraded, except for fertilizers, which are imported with a small import tax and some handling and transport charges. Extra demand for fertilizer, as well as extra demand for other agricultural inputs, is valued at their cost of supply converted to economic values. The investment costs are a mixture of imported equipment and materials together with nontraded materials sourced locally, and labor that is surplus in the area. The institutional support costs are dominated by international consultants with a small expenditure on domestic consultants and office services. The O&M costs are predominantly labor costs, with some input of imported parts for equipment and nontraded construction materials.

Table A16.2: Cost Breakdown and Conversion Factors

	Cost Breakdown (%)				
	Foreign Exchange	Labor	Nontraded Goods	Conversion Factors[a]	Foreign Exchange
Rice	80			20	1.26
Vegetables				100	1.00
Fertilizers	80		10	10	1.16
Labor		100			0.80
Other				100	1.00
Investment	50	30	5	15	1.06
O&M	10	60		30	0.91
Institutional Support	80	10		10	1.24
Conversion Factors	1.33	0.80		0.00	1.00

O&M = operation and maintenance.
[a] Conversion factors (CFs) using domestic price numeraire. They are weighted averages of the CFs for the four resource categories.
Source: ADB Economic Research and Regional Cooperation Department.

6.　　The cost breakdown of financial price values have been used, together with the shadow exchange rate factor and the shadow wage rate factor, to derive a conversion factor for each project item. These are also shown in Table A16.2. At the domestic price level, several of the conversion factor values are above 1.0, showing mainly that the foreign exchange they use or save is worth more to the national economy than is given by the official exchange rate. On the other hand, the labor component of project items is revalued downward by the shadow wage rate factor, which represents the opportunity cost of labor.

7.　　These conversion factors can be applied to the estimates of agricultural net output with and without the project. It is anticipated that input costs per ton will rise for irrigated rice production compared with unirrigated, as more labor time, fertilizers, and related costs are required, while inputs into vegetable production per ton will remain the same in quantitative terms without and with the project. For simplicity, the same input coefficients per ton of rice are assumed in the with and without project scenario.

8.　　Table A16.3 shows the effect of converting to economic prices for agricultural production in the without and with project cases. Despite lower economic prices than financial prices, the economic cost of rice production rises because of higher input use with the project. This is partly compensated for by the higher value given to rice output at economic prices. Nevertheless, the economic net output per ton of rice is less with the project than without the project. The project rice benefits come from the increase in area, cropping intensity and yield which the irrigation rehabilitation brings about. At the domestic price level, the nontraded vegetable output is valued the same at economic and financial prices. However, the economic cost of inputs into vegetable production is less than their financial cost and so there is an improvement in economic net output per ton and per hectare.

Table A16.3: Net Agricultural Output at Economic Prices
(Rs per ton)

Inputs	Rice Without Project Case		Rice With Project Case		Vegetables	
	Financial	Economic	Financial	Economic	Financial	Economic
Fertilizer	100	116	600	696	0	0
Labor	300	240	400	320	600	480
Other	600	600	700	700	300	300
Total Inputs	1,000	956	1,700	1,718	900	780
Output	6,335	8,007	6,335	8,007	3,000	3,000
Net Output	5,335	7,051	4,635	6,289	2,100	2,220

Rs = rupees.
Note: Economic values in national currency at the domestic price level.
Source: ADB Economic Research and Regional Cooperation Department.

9.   These net output estimates at economic prices are used, together with the project investment and O&M costs at economic prices, to derive the project economic statement at economic prices. Project economic costs and benefits are shown in Table A16.4. The project costs include the investment and O&M costs. It has also been assumed that one-tenth of irrigated and nonirrigated production will also be lost as a result of implementation activities. The project benefits include the agricultural net output with the project less the agricultural net output without the project, together with the saving in without project O&M costs.

10.   Only one other adjustment that is taken into account. For both the rice output and the fertilizer input, there is expected to be a change in relative price in the next few years. The real price of rice is expected to fall by about 26% over the next 10 years. Over the same period, the real price of fertilizer is expected to rise by about 8%. Both estimates are taken from the World Bank Commodity Price projections. Taken together, these imply a decline in the value of net output of rice at economic prices that will in part offset the increases in cropping intensity, rice area, and yields. These forecast changes in real prices have been used to adjust the estimate of incremental net output from rice production over the first 10 years of the project.

11.   The economic internal rate of return calculated in Table A16.4 is 16.2%. This rehabilitation project is not a marginal project. In Appendix 19, this basic EIRR is subject to sensitivity analysis.

Table A16.4: Project Economic Statement:
Irrigation Rehabilitation Project
(economic values using domestic price numeraire)

	Years							
	0	1	2	3	4	5	6	7–28[a]
Rice Price Forecast Factor	1.000	0.879	0.782	0.774	0.763	0.755	0.744	0.741
Fertilizer Price Forecast Factor	1.000	1.017	1.042	1.058	1.075	1.016	1.108	1.083
Costs (Rs million)								
Investment	553.9	553.9	553.9					
Institutional Support	94.8	94.8	94.8					
O&M				7.2	7.2	7.2	7.2	7.2
Total Costs	648.7	648.7	648.7	7.2	7.2	7.2	7.2	7.2
Benefits (Rs million)								
With Project (Net Output)								
Rice				868.9	1,358.9	1,689.7	1,630.1	1,627.5
Vegetables				140.7	225.1	281.4	268.4	281.4
Without Project (Net Output)								
Rice	121.0	104.3	91.0	898.3	882.8	873.0	856.0	852.4
Vegetables	42.7	42.7	42.7	427.4	427.4	427.4	427.4	427.4
Without Project O&M				9.1	9.1	9.1	9.1	18.3
Total Benefits	(163.7)	(147.1)	(133.7)	(306.9)	283.0	679.9	637.2	647.4
Net Benefits	(812.4)	(795.8)	(782.4)	(314.1)	275.8	672.7	630.0	640.2
Net Present Value at 9%	1,990							
EIRR	16.2%							

() = negative, EIRR = economic internal rate of return, O&M = operation and maintenance, Rs = rupees.
[a] Some values change annually up to year 10.
Source: ADB Economic Research and Regional Cooperation Department.

Appendix 17:
Illustration of Least-Cost
and Cost-Effectiveness Analysis

A.   Water Supply Project Alternatives

1.   Where alternatives offer different ways of producing a good or service of the same quality choice can be based on a comparison of costs per unit, with both costs and quantity of output discounted at the minimum required discount rate. Under many circumstances, the average incremental economic cost (AIEC) can be used to compare alternatives of different scale. Selecting the least-cost option through a comparison of the AIECs can be illustrated by the following example.

2.   Table A17.1 presents the cost streams of two alternative water supply projects where the source of water for alternative 1 is surface water while alternative 2 involves drilling for groundwater. Both offer the same water quantity. At a discount rate of 9%, alternative 1 is selected, being the least-cost option as indicated by the lower AIEC of Rs2.73/cubic meter (m^3) as opposed to Rs2.88/m^3.

Table A17.1: Choosing Project Alternatives Using
Average Incremental Economic Cost

| | Alternative 1: Surface Water | | | | Alternative 2: Groundwater | | | |
Year	Capital + O&M Rs'000s	Other Costs Rs'000s	Total Costs Rs'000s	Water Output '000s m^3	Capital + Q&M Rs'000s	Other Costs Rs'000s	Total Costs Rs'000s	Water Output '000s m^3
0	3,000	0	3,000	0	5,500	0	5,500	0
1	2,000	0	2,000	0	200	0	200	0
2	300	30	330	258	200	40	240	258
3	300	31	331	268	200	42	242	268
4	300	32	332	279	200	44	244	279
5	300	34	334	290	200	45	245	290
6	300	35	335	302	200	46	246	302
7	300	36	336	314	200	48	248	314
8	300	38	338	326	200	49	249	326
9	300	39	339	340	200	51	251	340
10	300	41	341	353	200	52	252	353
11	300	43	343	367	200	54	254	367
12	300	44	344	382	200	56	256	382

continued on next page

Table A17.1. continued

	Alternative 1: Surface Water				Alternative 2: Groundwater			
Year	Capital + O&M Rs'000s	Other Costs Rs'000s	Total Costs Rs'000s	Water Output '000s m³	Capital + Q&M Rs'000s	Other Costs Rs'000s	Total Costs Rs'000s	Water Output '000s m³
13	300	46	346	397	200	57	257	397
14	300	48	348	413	200	59	259	413
15	300	50	350	430	200	61	261	430
16	300	52	352	447	200	63	263	447
17	300	54	354	465	200	65	265	465
18	300	56	356	483	200	67	267	483
19	300	58	358	503	200	70	270	503
20	300	61	361	523	200	72	272	523
Present value at 9%			7,622	2,794			8,039	2,794
AIEC at 9% 2.73								2.88

AIEC = average incremental economic cost, m³ = cubic meter, O&M = operation and maintenance,
Rs = rupees.
ª All costs expressed in economic terms at constant prices.
Source: ADB Economic Research and Regional Cooperation Department.

3.   The comparison using the AIEC is straightforward where project alternatives deliver the same benefits and the discount rate is given. However, often the selection of the least-cost alternative will vary with the discount rate. Where the discount is uncertain, the equalizing (or crossover) discount rate between each pair of mutually exclusive options can be estimated. The equalizing discount rate is the rate at which the present values of the two cost streams are equal and, hence, is the discount rate at which the preference for one alternative over the other changes. It can be calculated as the rate at which the annual difference in costs between the alternatives becomes zero (that is, the internal rate of return [IRR] of the incremental cost stream). Table A17.2 illustrates for two alternative power plants, one with higher capital cost but lower operating cost.

Table A17.2: Choosing Project Alternatives Using the Equalizing Discount Rate

Year	Alternative 1: Geothermal Capital + O&M	Present Value[a] 8%	13%	Alternative 2: Coal-Fired Capital + O&M	Present Value[a] 8%	13%	Difference in Cost Streams
0	200	200	200	150	150	150	50
1	3,000	2,778	2,655	150	139	133	2,850
2	9,000	7,716	7,048	4,500	3,858	3,524	4,500
3	16,000	12,701	11,089	9,800	7,780	6,792	6,200
4	20,000	14,701	12,266	13,000	955	7,973	7,000
5	8,000	5,445	4,342	11,900	8,099	6,459	(3,900)
6	8,000	5,041	3,843	7,500	4,726	3,602	500
7	1,370	799	582	4,690	2,737	1,994	(3,320)
8	1,370	740	515	4,690	2,534	1,764	(3,320)
9	1,370	685	456	4,690	2,346	1,561	(3,320)
10	1,370	635	404	4,690	2,172	1,382	(3,320)
11	1,370	588	357	4,690	2,011	1,223	(3,320)
12	1,370	544	316	4,690	1,862	1,082	(3,320)
13	1,370	504	280	4,690	1,725	958	(3,320)
14	1,370	466	248	4,690	1,597	847	(3,320)
15	1,370	432	219	4,690	1,478	750	(3,320)
16	1,370	400	194	4,690	1,369	664	(3,320)
17	1,370	370	172	4,690	1,268	587	(3,320)
18	1,370	343	152	4,690	1,174	520	(3,320)
19	1,370	317	134	4,690	1,087	460	(3,320)
20	1,370	294	119	4,690	1,006	407	(3,320)
Total		55,699	45,590		58,673	42,831	
Incremental IRR							10.1%

( ) = negative, IRR = internal rate of return, O&M = operation and maintenance.
[a] Costs streams are expressed in economic terms at constant prices.
Source: ADB Economic Research and Regional Cooperation Department.

4.   A geothermal power plant with an aggregate capacity of 880 megawatts (MW) in 16 units of 55 MW each is being considered. The most technically feasible project alternative is a 900-megawatt coal-fired plant in 3 units of 300 MW each. The coal-fired plant has a little more capacity than the geothermal plant, but allowing for plant factors and transmission losses, the net power generation is treated as the same. While capital outlays for the geothermal project are higher and start earlier than the coal project due to the greenfield development, its operating costs are lower. The coal plant's recurrent costs are much higher due to its coal inputs.

5.   Table A17.2 presents the present worth of both project options at discount rates of 8% and 13%. The ranking of the geothermal and coal alternatives, based on the cost stream with the lowest present value, changes between the lower and higher discount rates. If the test rate is 8%, the geothermal project is selected. On the other hand, if it is 13%, the coal-fired project with the lower investment is the least-cost option. The equalizing discount rate at which the switchover occurs is estimated at 10%. If a test rate of 12% is used, the additional costs of the geothermal alternative are not worthwhile and the coal-fired alternative should be chosen.

B.   Health Project Alternatives

6.   In situations where a project has impacts that are difficult to value in monetary terms, the choice between alternatives needs to be based on measuring impact in some quantitative way and then comparing the cost of achieving that impact between alternatives. Here, the purpose of cost-effectiveness analysis is to find the project that minimizes resource use to achieve the desired results or that gives the maximum results for a given budget. This type of analysis is applied most frequently in the education and health sectors when it is difficult to put economic prices on educational or health effects. Here, impact may be in terms of a measure of educational attainment like literacy rates or of health outcomes like days of good health saved.

7.   The application of this form of least-cost analysis requires that a diverse set of impacts be expressed in a common unit of measurement, which can be compared with project costs. For example, health projects can affect both morbidity and mortality, and impacts will vary depending upon the characteristics of patients and the health conditions that are addressed. Cost-effectiveness analysis involves the calculation of the ratio of project cost to net health impacts measured in a common unit. This can be done simply on the basis of annual average costs and impact or alternatively looking at the profile of costs and impact over time and discounting both to the present. Where project alternatives are compared, the preferred option will have the lower cost per unit of impact.

8.   The unit used to measure health impacts is often the disability adjusted life years (DALY).[1] This takes account of the duration of an illness, its severity, and the ages of those affected. For each intervention, it will be necessary to estimate DALYs saved per 1,000 of population, taking account of factors like the incidence of a disease, its average age of onset, its average duration, its fatality and morbidity rates, and the effectiveness of the intervention in reducing incidence. For project

---

[1]   An explanation of the concept of DALYs and an illustration of their use in economic analysis of health projects are given in ADB. 2000. *Handbook for the Economic Analysis of Health Sector Projects*. Manila.

alternatives with data on the population covered, this will allow an estimate of health impact. Once this is available, a time profile of costs and impact over the life of an intervention can be set out and a choice made based on the lowest cost per DALY.

9.   Table A17.3 illustrates the use of cost-effectiveness for a comparison of projects to address the health conditions of meningitis and schistosomiasis. Both projects reach the same target population. The meningitis project is lower in cost but has a lower impact on DALYs saved, only 20 per 1,000, compared with 64 per 1,000 for the schistosomiasis project. The cost-effectiveness comparison is shown for three discount rates: 12%, 9%, and 3%. The cost-effectiveness measure for the meningitis project at 9% is $39.40/DALY, while the more expensive but higher impact schistosomiasis project is more cost-effective with a cost of approximately $27.29/DALY.

Table A17.3: Cost Effectiveness: Two Health Projects

Year	Meningitis			Schistosomiasis		
	Project Cost ($ million)	Population Reached ('000s)	DALY Saved	Project Cost ($ million)	Population Reached	DALY Saved
1	100	95	1,900	310	95	6,080
2	80	95	1,900	330	95	6,080
3	75	95	1,900	65	95	6,080
4	75	95	1,900	65	95	6,080
5	73	95	1,900	65	95	6,080
6	3	16	320	8	16	1,024
7	3	17	340	8	17	1,088
8	3	17	340	8	17	1,088
9	3	18	360	8	18	1,152
10	3	18	360	8	18	1,152
PV at 12%	301.7		7,548	680.68		24,154
PV at 9%	325.2		8,255	720.87		26,428
PV at 3%	382.6		10,058	816.94		32,185
CER[a] at 12%		39.96[b]			28.18	
CER[a] at 9%		39.39			27.29	
CER[a] at 3%		38.04			25.38	

CER = cost-effectiveness ratio, DALY = disability adjusted life years, PV = present value.
[a] CER is cost-effectiveness ratio in cost per DALY.
[b] Cost per DALY is the ratio of discounted cost to discounted DALYs divided by 1,000. For example, 301.7/ (7,548/1,000) = 39.96. Units for discounted cost are in millions of US dollars, so DALY figure of 7,548 must be converted to millions by division by 1,000.
Source: ADB Economic Research and Regional Cooperation Department.

10.   Health projects are often analyzed at a discount rate, which reflects society's time preference for consumption rather than opportunity cost on the grounds that they should not be treated as competing for the same funds as other projects. The comparison is also given at a 3% discount rate. The decision remains the same as the schistosomiasis project is still the more cost-effective, and the gap between the two alternatives has widened when a lower discount rate is used, due to the higher capital-intensity of the schistosomiasis project.

Appendix 18:
Estimating the National Economic
Discount Rate

A.   Methodology

1.   Typically, the time profile of accrual of project costs and benefits is different, with investment costs staggered at the beginning of the appraisal period, and benefits and operation and maintenance costs spread out over the life of a project. To calculate the net benefits, benefits and costs have to be made comparable by converting them into a present value. Doing so requires the use of a discount rate, which in the context of cost–benefit analysis is termed the social discount rate (SDR).

Two concepts of the social discount rate

2.   Broadly, two concepts have been advanced in the literature to estimate the SDR: one from the perspective of investor (demand price) and the other from the perspective of savers (supply price). According to the first, capital and other resources allocated to a public sector project have an alternative use where they can generate returns and, thus, these resources have an opportunity cost. Efficiency dictates that the proposed project should go ahead only if the rate of return from the public investment is at least as high as the return from the next best alternative use of the funds in the private sector. In this view, the SDR should be the marginal rate of return on private investment. In the absence of market distortions, the latter is equal to the marginal rate of return on private investment, also called the marginal social opportunity cost (SOC).

3.   The second concept assumes that consumers (savers) prefer to consume today rather than in the future. This is due to two reasons. One is that individuals expect their consumption to increase in the future and, hence, marginal utility of consumption will fall. Therefore, for every unit of consumption sacrificed today, more than one will have to be given in return in the future. Second, even if individuals value consumption in the future as they do today, the rate of time preference is positive because they are impatient and/or there is a risk of not being alive tomorrow. In this view, the SDR is the marginal social rate of time preference (SRTP), i.e., the rate at which the society is willing to postpone a marginal unit of consumption in exchange for more future consumption.

4.   In an economy with no distortions and perfect competition, the market rate of interest equates demand for and supply of investible funds and the demand price (SOC) and supply price (SRTP) are equal. The market interest rate thus determines the SDR. In reality, however, there are distortions due to, for example, taxes on corporate earnings and on individuals' interest income, externalities, information asymmetry, or risks. These imperfections create a wedge between the SRTP and SOC, making both deviate from the market interest rate.

Two practical estimation methods

5.   In practice, two alternative methods have been used in estimating the SDR. One is the weighted average method, which attempts to reconcile the two concepts of SDR discussed above. The method recognizes that the funds available to public projects may come from various sources—displaced private investment, foregone consumption today, or borrowing from international capital markets. The SDR is thus a weighted average of SOC, the SRTP, and the cost of international borrowing inclusive of the risk premium. If, however, the country faces credit rationing in global markets, demand for new funds to finance a public sector project will be met only from foregone domestic consumption and displaced private investment. The SDR in such a scenario will be the weighted average of SOC and the SRTP.

6.   Central to the estimation of SDR using the weighted cost of capital approach are the weights to be assigned to the three components—the SRTP, SOC, and the foreign borrowing rate. Typically, these weights are derived from estimates of the elasticity of domestic savings, investment, and foreign supply of funds with respect to the discount rate. Thus, the SDR is estimated as follows:

$$\delta = \alpha\rho + \beta r + (1-\alpha-\beta)\,MCF \qquad\qquad (1)$$

Where, δ denotes the SDR, ρ is the SOC, r is the SRTP, MCF is the marginal economic cost of foreign borrowing, α is the proportion of funds for public investment diverted from private investment, β is the proportion of funds diverted from current consumption, and $(1-\alpha-\beta)$ is the proportion of funds that come from foreign borrowing. Expressed in terms of the elasticities of demand and supply, Equation 1 can be rewritten as:

$$\delta = \frac{\varepsilon_r\,(S_r/S_t)r + \varepsilon_f\,(S_f/St)MCF - \varepsilon_j\,(I_t/S_t)\rho}{\varepsilon_r\,(S_r/S_t) + \varepsilon f\,(S_f/S_t) - \varepsilon j\,(I_t/(S_t))} \qquad\qquad (2)$$

Where, ε_r, ε_f , and ε_j are respectively the elasticities of domestic savings, foreign capital, and private investment with respect to the interest rate. (S_r/S_t) and (S_f/S_t) are the shares of domestic (S_r) and foreign savings (net foreign capital inflows) (S_f) in total savings (S_t), respectively. (I_t/S_t) is the ratio of private sector investment (I_t) to savings.

7.   The weighted average approach has been considered as a preferred method for empirical estimation of the SDR as it explicitly considers market imperfections and credit constraints on investment.[1] However, this method requires information on a number of variables. Where information is unavailable, assumptions have to be made, with the resulting SDR estimates becoming very sensitive to the assumptions used.

8.   The other practical method for estimating the SDR is to use the so-called Ramsey formula, also called the Ramsey method or "optimal growth rate method". This method does not reply on market interest rates; instead, it states that in an optimal inter-temporal allocation of resources, the productivity of capital (or the discount rate) is equal to the SRTP, and is the sum of the rate of pure time preference (describing impatience) and the product of the consumption elasticity of marginal utility (describing how fast marginal utility decreases with consumption) and growth rate of per capita real consumption (describing how fast consumption increases), that is,

$$SDR = SRTP = r = \mu + \theta \times g \tag{3}$$

Where r is interest rate, μ is pure rate of time preference, θ is the elasticity of marginal utility of consumption, and g is annual rate of growth of per capita real consumption.

9.   Using the Ramsey method to estimate the SDR thus requires estimates of the three components: μ, θ, and g. Growth of per capita real consumption can be approximated with the growth rate of real GDP per capita, data on which are relatively easy to collect. However, choice of μ and θ is more difficult and has been the subject of intense debate. A survey of empirical estimates of μ shows that the estimated range is

---

[1]   For empirical applications, see Zhuang, J., Z. Liang, T. Lin, and F. De Guzman. 2007. *Theory and Practice in the Choice of Social Discount Rate for Cost–Benefit Analysis: A Survey*. ERD Working Paper. No. 94. ADB; Jenkins, G. P., C-Y. Kuo, A.C. Harberger. 2011. *The Economic Opportunity Cost of Capital. Development Discussion Paper No. 2011-8*. Queen's University; and Harberger, A. C. and G. P. Jenkins. 2015. *Musings on the Social Discount Rate. Development Discussion Paper No. 2015-01*. Queen's University.

1%–3%.[2] The Government of the United Kingdom in its The Green Book,[3] adopts a value of 1.5%. For European Union countries, the empirical estimates of μ range from a low of 0.63% in Ireland to 1.29% in Hungary, with an average of 0.94%.[4]

10.   Empirical estimates of the elasticity of the marginal utility of consumption, , also vary from one study to another. A survey of the literature shows that the estimated range is 1–2.[5] The UK government in its The Green Book: Appraisal and Evaluation in Central Government adopts a value of 1.[6] For 20 European Union countries, the estimate ranges from a low of 1.09 in Poland to 2.31 in Ireland, with an average over 20 countries of 1.50.[7]

11.   Compared to the weighted average method, the Ramsey method is relatively easier to implement as it involves only three variables and is less demanding on data. However, it is based on the strong assumption of an optimal inter-temporal allocation of resources and the absence of credit constraints on investment in an economy, so there is no overall shortage of savings to fund new investment.

B.   Choice of the Social Discount Rate in ADB

12.   Asian Development Bank has been using an ADB-wide default SDR, or the minimum required economic internal rate of return of 12%. ADB will now use a revised new default rate of 9%. The revision takes into consideration continued increases in the income levels of developing Asia, lower foreign borrowing costs compared with the past, and the growing importance of environment protection projects in ADB lending that tend to have very long-term impacts, all suggesting a lower SDR.

13.   The new default rate is calculated using the Ramsey method with the following assumptions: (i) $\mu = 1$; (ii) $\theta = 1.5$; and (iii) $g = 5$%, which is the projected gross domestic product (GDP) per capita growth for 2016–2030 for developing Asia. Collating these values gives an SDR of 8.5% (= 1 + 1.5 × 5.0), which is rounded up off to 9%.

[2]   See Zhuang, J., Z. Liang, T. Lin, and F. De Guzman. 2007. Theory and Practice in the Choice of Social Discount Rate for Cost–Benefit Analysis: A Survey. ERD Working Paper. No. 94.
[3]   HM Treasury. 2003. The Green Book: Appraisal and Evaluation in Central Government. HM Treasury.
[4]   Florio, M. and E. Sirtori. 2013. The Social Cost Of Capital: Recent Estimates for the EU Countries. Working Paper No. 03/2013. Centre for Industrial Studies.
[5]   Zhuang, J., Z. Liang, T. Lin, T. and F. De Guzman. 2007. Theory and Practice in the Choice of Social Discount Rate for Cost–Benefit Analysis: A Survey. ERD Working Paper. No. 94. ADB.
[6]   HM Treasury. 2003. The Green Book: Appraisal and Evaluation in Central Government. HM Treasury.
[7]   Florio, M. and E. Sirtori. 2013. The Social Cost of Capital: Recent Estimates for the EU Countries. Working Paper No. 03/2013. Centre for Industrial Studies.

14. However, when there are strong reasons to suggest that the ADB-wide default SDR is not relevant for a particular developing member country, a country specific SDR can be estimated using either the weighted average or Ramsey approach, with justifications clearly explained. The same SDR should be applied consistently to all the projects in the same developing member country.

15. A lower discount rate of 6% can be applied as the minimum required economic internal rate of return for social sector projects, selected poverty targeting projects (such as rural roads and rural electrification), and projects that primarily generate environmental benefits (such as pollution control, protection of the ecosystem, flood control, and control of deforestation). The application of a lower social discount rate to such projects can be justified on the following considerations: (i) social sector projects and poverty-targeting projects often have significant unquantifiable benefits; and (ii) many environmental protection and conservation projects have very long-term impacts which justify a lower discount rate. When the lower rate is used, a clear rationale should be provided.

Appendix 19:
Treatment of Uncertainty:
Sensitivity and Risk Analysis

A. Sensitivity Analysis: Irrigation Project

1.   The irrigation rehabilitation project example of Appendix 17 is used here to illustrate the application of sensitivity analysis. The project involves a predicted increase in cropped area for irrigated rice, in cropping intensity, and in yield, as a result of irrigation rehabilitation, with a compensating decline in vegetable-cropped area. The base case result, economic internal rate of return of 16.2% and economic net present value of Rs1,990 million at 9% discount rate, is also based on a long-term relative economic price decline for rice and a long-term relative economic price increase for fertilizer. The main variables to which the base case may be sensitive, together with the possible changes in those variables, are selected as follows.

2.   On the basis of previous rehabilitation projects, there is uncertainty over the farmers' response to improved irrigation. Evaluation studies indicate the possibility of lower values for cropped rice area by 9%, cropping intensity by 10%, and yield by 6%. There is also uncertainty over the levels of cropping intensity and yield of both vegetables and rice, without the project. Increases in these variables of 10% have been included in the sensitivity tests.

3.   The forecast price of rice and fertilizer should be key variables in the project analysis, as the project will increase both the quantity of rice output and the quantity of fertilizer input. In the sensitivity analysis, the forecast price of rice, which declines over the first 10 years of the project anyway, is tested at a 20% lower level each year. On a similar basis, the fertilizer price is tested at a price 20% higher than in the base case.

4.   Other variables are also included in the sensitivity analysis. There have been delays in implementing previous projects. A 2-year delay is considered here. The effect of a 10% higher investment cost is also tested. The project benefits depend upon continued maintenance activities. Rather than a higher level of maintenance costs, the last 5 operating years of the project are excluded to allow for the possibility of inadequate maintenance activity. The value of the shadow exchange rate factor is also tested for the impact of a 10 percentage point change. Finally, some possible combinations of variables are also tested. These are a 2-year delay and a 10% investment cost increase, and a 5-year fall in the working life of the project and a 6% drop in yields.

5.   The results of these sensitivity tests on underlying and specific benefit and cost factors are given in Table A19.1. By observing the switching values in each case, very large changes are required in some variables for the project decision to change. This includes investment costs, the economic price of fertilizer, and the yield for vegetables. For some other variables, such as cropping intensity, yield for rice without the project, and the reduced operating life because of inadequate maintenance, not so large but still unlikely differences from the base case would have to occur for the project decision to change.

6.   There are some variables to which the project is most sensitive and to which most attention should be paid. These are the economic price of rice, and the cropping intensity and the yield for rice with the project. The switching value for the rice price is a reduction of 23% below the long-run forecast value. The switching value for the rice area, cropping intensity, and yield with the project is 17% for each. The world price of rice is outside the control of the producers and the country. However, area planted under rice, cropping intensity, and yields are part of the project design and implementation process, which the executing agency can affect to some degree. It will be critical to ensure that farmers have the incentive to behave as predicted in the project design.

7.   The project result is also sensitive to delays in implementation, particularly if delays are combined with an increase in investment costs. With a 2-year delay, it takes only a 22% increase in investment costs in real terms to render the project marginal. In addition, if poor maintenance shortens the project life by 5 years, it takes only a 12% drop in rice yields to make the project marginal. Both delays and cost increases and maintenance are at least in part within the control of the project management unit.

8.   In economic pricing, the assumed large undervaluation of foreign exchange implied by a shadow exchange rate factor of 1.33 would have to be replaced by an overvaluation to have an impact on the project result.

Table A19.1: Results of Sensitivity Analysis: Irrigation Rehabilitation Project

Item	Change (%)	ENPV (Rs million)	EIRR (%)	Sensitivity Indicator[d]	Switching Value (%)
Base case		880			
At 9%		1,990	16.2		
Costs					
Investment costs	+10.0	1,826	15.3	0.83	121
Fertilizer, economic price	+20.0	1,601	14.9	0.98	102
Benefits					
Rice economic price	(20.0)	269	10.1	(4.32)	(23)
With:					
Rice area	(9)	927.8	12.6	(5.93)	(17)
Rice cropping intensity	(10)[a]	810	14.0	(5.93)	(17)
Rice yield	(6)	1,282	13.8	(5.94)	(17)
Without:					
Rice cropping intensity	+ 10[a]	1,330	13.9	3.32	30
Rice yield	+ 10	1,330	13.9	3.32	30
Vegetables yield	+ 10	1,652	15.0	1.70	59
Delay in benefits				NPV at 9% declines by	
Two years		1,263	13.2	37%	
Operating life				NPV declines by	
Reduced 5 years		1,675	15.8	16%	
Shadow price factors					
SERF	(10)[a]	1,579	14.9	(2.07)	(48)[a]
Combinations					
A. Investment cost and 2-year delay	+ 10	1,098.7	12.5	4.48	22[b]
B. Lower rice yield and 5-year shorter life	(6)	1,015.2	13.3	(8.17)	(12)[c]

( ) = negative, EIRR = economic internal rate of return, ENPV = economic net present value, NPV = net present value, Rs = rupees, SERF = shadow exchange rate factor.
[a] Percentage point change.
[b] Switching value of investment cost with 2-year delay.
[c] Switching value of crop yields with shorter working life.
[d] Percentage change in ENPV over percentage change in variable as a whole number.
Source: ADB Economic Research and Regional Cooperation Department.

9. These results of the sensitivity analysis suggest considerable risk because the project returns are so dependent on rice production and there is a great degree of uncertainty about the future economic price of rice, which is outside the project's control. In addition, the domestic price for rice and the rice marketing system should be reviewed to ensure there is sufficient financial incentive for farmers to switch from vegetable to rice production in the early project years, otherwise the economic benefits of the project will be delayed. Finally there needs to be close adherence to the project planning and maintenance schedule to minimize delay and increases in investment cost and ensure that higher yields are sustained.

B.   Risk Analysis: Road Project Illustration

10. The application of risk analysis is illustrated for a road improvement project.[1] Project benefits are determined by the growth of traffic on the road and the savings in vehicle operating costs as a result of the road improvement. Traffic flow with and without the project is forecast by a model combining the effects of the growth of income (through an income elasticity demand for travel and a gross domestic product growth projection) and a reduction in user cost for the road (through a price elasticity of demand for travel). The key aspects of vehicle costs are fuel, vehicle depreciation, and the cost of driver and passenger time. The main element of project cost is the capital cost of road improvement.

11. Table A19.2 gives the main results of a sensitivity analysis of the project. The switching value for capital cost is 54%, and for the fuel price it is a fall of 29%. The project is critically sensitive to the assumed income growth with a switching value of 2.7% annually.

Table A19.2: Road Project Sensitivity Analysis

	Change	ENPV	EIRR	Switching Value[a]
Base Case		66.96	17.3%	
Capital Cost	10%	54.58	16.0%	1.540
	20%	42.20	14.9%	
	30%	29.82	13.9%	
Fuel	(20%)	47.86	15.8%	0.291
	(10%)	57.39	16.6%	
	10%	76.56	17.9%	
	20%	86.19	18.6%	
	30%	95.86	19.3%	

continued on next page

---

[1] This example comes from Chapter 7 of ADB. 2013. *Cost–Benefit Analysis for Development: A Practical Guide.* The illustration uses a 12% discount rate.

Table A19.2. continued

	Change	ENPV	EIRR	Switching Value[a]
Income Growth	1.02	(9.84)	10.90%	1.027
	1.10	217.90	23.8%	
Price Elasticity	(0.90)	109.31	20.1%	0.63
	(0.10)	36.37	15.0%	

( ) = negative, EIRR = economic internal rate of return, ENPV = economic net present value.
[a] Switching values for capital cost and fuel are percentages, 54% and 9%, respectively. Switching value for income growth is 2.7%. The switching value for price elasticity is 0.63 (as compared with –0.5 in the base case).
Source: ADB. 2013. *Cost–Benefit Analysis for Development: A Practical Guide*. Manila (Table 7.18).

12.   A risk analysis focuses on random changes in these key variables within a specified functional form with other variables held at their base case values. The four key variables—gross domestic product growth, price elasticity for travel, fuel price, and capital cost—are varied randomly and simultaneously using a random number generator following a normal distribution within a chosen range with the base case values defining the mean. Table A19.3 gives the parameters and the range within which they vary.

Table A19.3: Road Project: Parameter Variation

Parameter	Range (Base Case)
GDP growth, annual	2% to 10% (6%)
Price elasticity	–0.9 to -0.1 (–0.5)
Capital cost	–20% to +20% of base case
Fuel price	–50% to +50% of base case

( ) = negative, GDP = gross domestic product.
Source: ADB. 2013. *Cost–Benefit Analysis for Development: A Practical Guide*. Manila (Table 7.19).

13.   The resulting expected value, that is, the probability weighted economic net present value (ENPV), is $72.57 million, approximately 8% higher than the base case. The results are shown graphically in Figure A19. The probability of project failure, defined by a negative ENPV is less than 5%. While there is no unique cut-off rate for acceptable risk levels at 5%, the project appears to be very low risk. Basing a decision on the expected ENPV means that the project is clearly acceptable.

Figure A19: Probability Distribution of Economic Net Present Value

Distribution for NPV

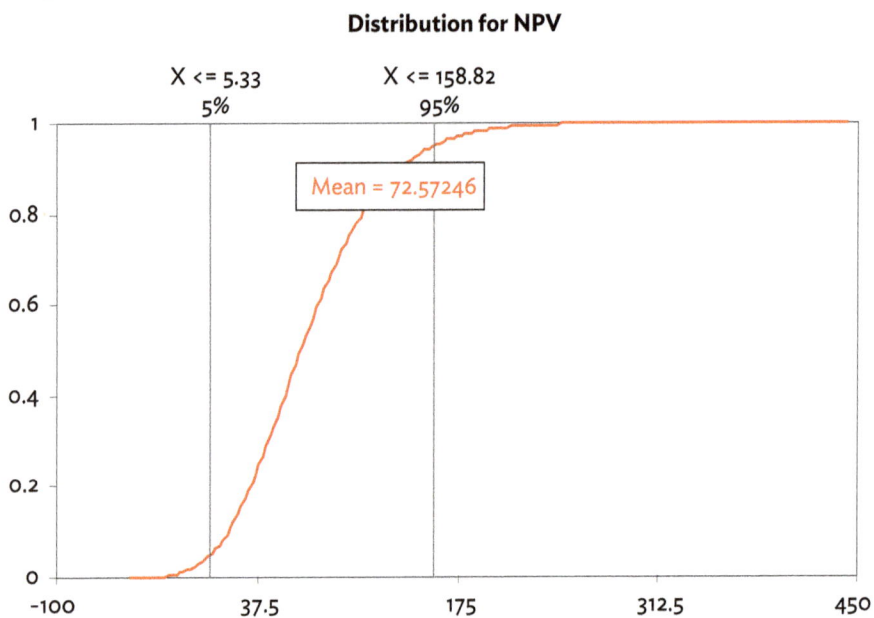

NPV = net present value.
Source: ADB Economic Research and Regional Cooperation Department.

Appendix 20:
Distribution of Project Effects

A.   Tracing Income Flows

1.   In revenue-generating projects, a project statement of costs and benefits at financial prices can be constructed to assess who gains and who loses from the financial transactions created by a project. In addition to these financial flows, the economic analysis will capture additional income or effects equivalent to changes in income not reflected in financial transactions.

2.   For a full distribution analysis incorporating economic effects, the identity of all the key groups that gain or lose, and the size of their gains and losses, need to be estimated. Different groupings of stakeholders or project participants are possible. A common simplified grouping is as follows:
   a.   the owners of the entity operating the project,
   b.   those working in the project,
   c.   the government,
   d.   the consumers of project outputs, and
   e.   those providing material inputs to the project.

3.   Under some circumstances, it may also be necessary to show the effects on project lenders (where interest rate subsidies are involved), foreign investors, and on parties from different countries in a region (see Appendix 15). The normal perspective on projects is the national economy, so the economic net present value (ENPV) captures gains to the economy that go to locally resident groups. A more detailed analysis will also subdivide the basic groups, for example, into different types of consumers (for example, those above or below the poverty line), workers (such as scarce or surplus labor), and households resettled as a result of a project or by gender.

4.   Income change created by a project is composed of income changes created by the financial flows associated with the project and measured by financial net present value (FNPV) and income changes created by any difference between economic and financial prices (ENPV – FNPV). The financial position of a project is the starting point for the analysis of its distribution effects since transactions at financial prices determine actual money flows. Thus, assuming that 12% represents the financial as well as the economic opportunity cost of capital, a positive FNPV before tax is a gain to investors and the government, which will collect profits tax, and correspondingly a negative FNPV is a loss to investors. More detailed analysis of the financial effects

of a project would need to incorporate a separate measure of financial opportunity costs for investors, but for practical purposes, as part of distribution analysis, the simplification of using 9% to reflect these costs can be applied.

5.   The second step is to account for the distribution of the economic benefits and costs, which are over and above financial benefits and costs. The differences between financial and economic costs and benefits also create income flows although not ones observed directly in financial transactions. These flows must be allocated to one of the different groups participating in the project. The use of domestic price units to measure economic prices enables income flows arising from the financial effects of a project to be added directly to income flows arising from the difference between economic and financial prices.[1] The discussion here focuses on the application of distribution analysis when the economic calculations use the domestic price numeraire.

6.   Whenever an economic price of a project item differs from its financial price, this will create an income change not reflected in the financial calculations. For example, if consumers are willing to pay more than they are actually charged, the economic price will be average willingness to pay and the difference between this and the actual financial price is consumer surplus or a gain to consumers. Similarly, if the economic price of labor, the shadow wage rate, is below the financial price, that is the wage, this will be a gain to labor since workers are being paid more than their estimated productivity and by assumption earnings in their alternative activity.

7.   Any subsidy or tax on a project input will create a difference between economic and financial prices. A subsidy means economic costs are below financial costs and the full cost of the item is less than what the project pays, so there is a loss to the economy not reflected in the FNPV. This loss is usually assumed to be borne by the government (unless taxes are raised to cover it in which case it is borne by taxpayers). Alternatively, a tax on an input means its economic price is below its financial price, since assuming supply is expanded to meet project demand, economic costs are less than financial costs by the extent of the tax, so there is an income gain not reflected in the FNPV. This is a gain to the government (unless other taxes are lowered in which case it is a gain for taxpayers).

8.   The macroeconomic parameter, the SERF, also affects distribution, since where the SERF is greater than unity this implies a premium on foreign exchange, so that foreign currency generated or used by a project is worth more than in the financial analysis. This means that the FNPV understates benefits if the project is a

---

[1]   If the world price numeraire is used in the economic analysis, a further step of multiplying financial flows by the SCF is required.

net generator of foreign exchange where its output is exported or replaces imports. On the other hand, the FNPV will overstate benefits if the project is a net user of foreign exchange. The reverse arguments hold where the SERF is below 1.0 and the domestic currency is undervalued and foreign currency is overvalued. These income changes are not reflected in the FNPV and the convention in this analysis is to allocate these income effects to the government, on the grounds that the sale of foreign currency to a project by the Central Bank at the official undervalued price for foreign currency is equivalent to a project subsidy, while the purchase of foreign currency from a project at this undervalued rate is equivalent to a tax.

9.   These adjustments allow an estimate of the first round effects of a project on distribution. For some projects, there may be important indirect effects, for example, arising from a reduction in costs being passed on to consumers or higher profits creating greater demand for labor and thus higher wages. Insofar as it is possible to estimate these second round effects, they should be allowed for. However, doing this accurately can be difficult. This means that distribution analysis is really most appropriate for poverty targeting projects where the aim is to provide goods or services directly to poor households and where indirect effects are anticipated to be relatively minor.

B.   A Water Project Illustration

10.   These procedures are illustrated based on the water project example from Appendix 13.[2] Table A20.1 gives the original data on the project at financial prices. An analysis of financial cost data of the project suggests the equipment component of capital cost is composed of 90% cost, insurance, and freight (CIF) price, 4.5% import duty, and 5.5% cost of local transport to the project. The cost of construction is composed of 40% surplus labor, 10% scarce labor, 30% nontraded materials, 10% imported traded materials, and 10% taxes. Estimates of operating costs suggest all labor is scarce (that is, it has other employment opportunities), fuel is 80% traded and 20% indirect taxes, and local parts and components are 80% nontraded and 20% taxes.

11.   The project is publicly funded and sells water below the price consumers are willing to pay. For simplicity, all of the funding is assumed to come directly from the government so that the negative financial NPV at 9% of $28.42 million is assumed to be borne solely by the government and funded from the government budget.

---

[2]   More detailed case studies are in Chapters 7 and 8 of ADB. 2013. *Cost–Benefit Analysis for Development: A Practical Guide.* Manila.

Table A20.1: Water Project Data: Financial Prices

		Years											
		1	2	3	4	5	6	7	8	9	10	11	12
Water		0	0	90	110	110	110	110	110	110	110	110	110
Capital													
Equipment		20	40										
Construction		30	60										
Operating													
Wages				25	25	25	25	25	25	25	25	25	25
Fuel				20	25	25	25	25	25	25	25	25	25
Materials				33.3	40	40	40	40	40	40	40	40	40
Total cost		50	100	78.3	90	90	90	90	90	90	90	90	90
Net		(50)	(100)	11.7	20	20	20	20	20	20	20	20	20
NPV	(28.42)												
IRR	4%												

( ) = negative, IRR = internal rate of return, NPV = net present value.
Source: ADB Economic Research and Regional Cooperation Department.

12.   For the economic valuation, a number of adjustments will create a divergence between financial and economic prices:
   a.   Willingness to pay for water is introduced with a premium of 15%.
   b.   All taxes on cost are excluded.
   c.   Surplus labor is employed in building the project, and labor costs in construction are adjusted by a conversion factor (CF) of 0.70 (implying opportunity costs are 70% of the wage paid). Scarce labor is not adjusted.
   d.   The exchange rate is estimated to be overvalued by 15% (SERF = 1.15).

13.   To introduce these adjustments, the benefits and costs of the project at financial prices are disaggregated into traded and nontraded items, surplus, and scarce labor and transfers. For the economic valuation, the economic value of water is taken as 15% above the tariff. This is a willingness-to-pay value, which is nontraded. The net effect of these adjustments is a difference between the ENPV and FNPV of $150.800 million. As the FNPV is minus $28.42 million, the expression is FNPV + (ENPV – FNPV) = $122.38 million, which is the ENPV.

14.   The distributional effect of the difference between the ENPV and the FNPV is determined by the combined effect of the coefficients for traded and nontraded items, surplus, and scarce labor and transfers, and the economic conversion factors assigned to these.

15.   Each project item needs to be examined to demonstrate the income effects implied by these adjustments. Wherever economic benefits exceed financial ones (as in the case of willingness to pay), there will be an income gain not reflected in the financial analysis and, similarly, where economic costs exceed financial costs (for example, as in the case of equipment) there will be an income loss not reflected in the financial analysis. Table A20.2 sets out the distribution results.

16.   Benefits: Willingness to pay has a 15% premium reflecting the fact that consumers on average are willing to pay 15% more than the tariff. This means that 15% of the financial price value of benefits of 86.81 (0.15 × 578.73) are a gain to consumers.

17.   Costs:
   a.   Equipment: 90% of equipment cost at financial prices is the import price, which is treated as all traded. As this is a foreign currency value converted at the prevailing exchange rate, it is adjusted by the 15% premium implied by the SERF of 1.15. The loss of a premium on foreign currency of 7.02 (0.9 × 49.74 × 0.15) is treated as a loss to the government as scarce foreign currency is sold to the project at an undervalued price. In addition, 4.5% of the equipment costs are taxes which go to the government, so the government gains 2.34 (0.045 × 52.02) of the cost as a partial offset to the foreign exchange premium. The net position for the government is −4.68. Note that in this case equipment costs are higher in economic than financial prices because of the SERF of 1.15, so there is loss of income not reflected in the financial calculations and this loss is borne by the government.
   b.   Construction: This cost is decomposed into traded and nontraded cost, both categories of labor and transfers. Nontraded costs and scarce labor have conversion factors (CFs) of 1.0 so they create no additional income change. Ten percent of construction costs are traded so the government loses the foreign exchange premium on these of 1.17 (0.10 × 78.02 × 0.15). Another 10% is taxes, so this is a gain to the government of 7.80 (0.10 × 78.02). Unskilled labor employed in construction is 40% of the cost and gains 30% of the wage paid as the SWRF is 0.7. The gain to labor is therefore 9.36 (0.4 × 78.02 × 0.3).
   c.   Wages: Project labor is all treated as workers in scarce supply whose wages equal their opportunity cost. For these workers there is no income effect as they are assumed to be able to find equivalent

Table A20.2: Distribution Results

	Financial Prices	Economic Prices	Difference	Government Traded	Transfers	Consumers Nontraded	Labor Scarce	Labor Surplus
Benefits								
Water	578.73	665.54	86.81			86.81		
Costs								
Capital								
Equipment	52.02	56.70	4.68	(7.02)	2.34			
Construction	78.02	62.02	(16.00)	(1.17)	7.80			9.36
Operating								
Wages	135.04	135.04	–					
Fuel	131.18	120.69	(10.49)	(15.74)	26.24			
Materials	210.89	168.71	42.18		42.18			
Total Costs	607.15	543.17						
Net Benefits	(28.42)	150.80	122.38	(23.93)	78.56	86.81	–	9.36
Summary:								

	Government	Consumers	Labor Surplus
Financial NPV	(28.42)	86.81	9.36
Economic – Financial NPV	54.63	86.81	9.36
Income Change	26.21	86.81	9.36

( ) = negative, NPV = net present value.
Source: ADB Economic Research and Regional Cooperation Department.

employment without the project.

d. Fuel: This is 80% a traded cost and, thus, the government loses the foreign exchange premium which is 15.74 (0.8 × 131.18 × 0.15). However, fuel has a tax component of 20% and this is a gain to the government of 26.24 (0.2 × 131.18).

e. Materials: These are largely nontraded costs but their 20% tax component creates a gain for the government of 42.18 (0.2 × 210.89).

18. The net effect of these adjustments means that there is a significant gain to the government of 54.63 composed of the tax gains offset against the losses of the foreign exchange premium. There is a large gain to consumers of 86.81 and smaller gain to unskilled construction workers of 9.36. These changes are then combined with the results from the financial analysis of –28.42 to give a net figure for the government of 26.21.

C. Impact on Poverty Reduction

19. Consideration of the social impact of a project including its poverty impact should be incorporated at the earliest stage of project planning so that the project's social consequences can be addressed in project design. Where a project is explicitly designed to target the poor, initial planning should

a. explain who the poor or other target groups served by the project are;

b. explain the mechanism by which the poor are affected, for example, as users or consumers of project output, as workers employed on the project, or as suppliers of inputs to the project;

c. set out the critical assumptions required for the project to achieve its desired impact; and

d. explain the risks involved, which could result in leakage to the non-poor or lack of uptake by the poor.

20. For poverty targeted projects, the current socioeconomic status of users and other project participants, like employees, will need to be established, either by collecting primary data or relying on available existing sources. The need or demand for project services by the target population must be assessed and, in some instances, it will be appropriate to conduct surveys to establish demand at different user charges and to estimate willingness to pay. For certain types of project, for example, village-based rural water and sanitation schemes, community participation in the design and maintenance of the schemes will be sought and the mechanism for this must be established.

21.   Distribution analysis can be used to highlight a project's impact on target groups, where an important project goal is to improve their position. A particular focus on net benefits going to the poor is pertinent to many agricultural, social sector, urban development, and public utility projects. For example, for agricultural projects, the benefits to producers can be broken down in headcount terms among farmers with different income levels and, similarly, in water projects headcount distribution among water consumers can be estimated. Where poverty targeting is a key objective, information about likely beneficiaries is part of the process of project identification and design, and not just of appraisal. For gender equity targeting projects it will be necessary to estimate the share of women and households headed by women in beneficiaries.

22.   Only specific types of projects will require information on poverty impact and this can be presented directly in terms of numbers of the poor reached and services provided. However, for some projects it is also useful to present monetary estimates of the gains to the poor and their share in the net benefits created by the project. A poverty impact ratio is the share of the ENPV going to the poor. Its estimation requires that a basic distribution analysis is complemented by estimates of the proportion of the gains (and losses) to each beneficiary group, which goes to the poor. On the assumption that the share of the poor in gains/losses to different groups is constant over the life of a project, the total net present value of income flows can be multiplied by the assumed proportions of gains/losses to the poor.

23.   The data from the water example can be used to illustrate the approach, where it is necessary to disaggregate the broad categories of consumers and workers, at least into those above and below the poverty line (Table A20.3). The share of the poor in benefits to consumers is estimated by separating consumers into those above and those below the poverty line and estimating a separate willingness to pay for the two groups, for example, from a contingent valuation survey. From a local survey, 83% of consumer households are found to be below the poverty line and 17% to be above.

24.   Estimated willingness to pay for the average poor household is 10% above the tariff (CF = 1.1) and for a non-poor household it is 40% above (CF = 1.4). Using the population share of the poor and non-poor groups as a weight gives the overall willingness-to-pay CF of 1.15 (0.83 × 1.1 + 0.17 × 1.4 = 1.15). The percentage share of the poor in total willingness-to-pay benefits is estimated as 0.83 times 1.1 divided by 1.15 = 0.79, which is rounded to 0.80.

Table A20.3: Poverty Impact Ratio

Group	Income Change	Share to the Poor	Income Change for the Poor
Consumers	86.81	0.80	69.45
Workers	9.36	0.30	2.81
Government	26.21	0.15	3.93
ENPV	122.38		
Total Poverty Impact			76.19
PIR			0.62

ENPV = economic net present value, PIR = poverty impact ratio.
Source: ADB Economic Research and Regional Cooperation Department.

25.   The share of wage gains to unskilled labor going to the poor is estimated at 30% based on a local labor market survey. Of government income received from the project, it is assumed that 15% will ultimately benefit the poor. This assumption is based on a review of government expenditure categories with social expenditure and earmarked poverty programs taken to benefit the poor directly.

26.   With these assumptions on the share of gains to the poor, the total poverty impact in terms of income change to the poor is 76.19, which is approximately 62% of the ENPV (76.19/122.38 = 0.6225). The important point of the illustration is that in this type of project it will be important to distinguish between different categories of beneficiaries by a form of survey, since the willingness to pay will differ between the poor and those above the poverty line.

www.ingramcontent.com/pod-product-compliance
Lightning Source LLC
Chambersburg PA
CBHW040137270326
41927CB00020B/3429